THE HUMAN EXPERIMENT
SUCCESS OR FAILURE?

A New Version of Our Human Story

by James M. Jeffrey

Foreword

To know the reason for titling this book "The Human Experiment: Success or Failure?" we must begin with our first human ancestors and see that they had inherited several new survival tools. These included a new type of brain structure which enabled persons to use *reason* to create cooperative ideas in their minds, plus the potential to develop the vocal language needed to share their ideas with each other in their small, food-gathering groups.

We do not know how much time and effort were required for them to develop their potential for speech, and to begin sharing their cooperative ideas, but we do know that eventually they succeeded.

This enabled them to take the first step toward beginning what is called in this book, "The Human Experiment." Its purpose was to see if by creating, sharing, and living according to *cooperative ideas*, they could improve their ability to survive and enjoy life in their dangerous natural surroundings, without having to depend wholly on instinct to guide them.

They were not yet evolved enough mentally to be able to know consciously about the foregoing. Nevertheless they learned quickly from experience what was good or bad for them, and quite naturally entered into the Experiment because they found that it was helping them.

....

Discovering whether or not The Experiment continued to be helpful has been central to this book, for two main reasons.

One reason is that my original purpose for researching and writing it was to fulfill a promise I made during WW II that, if I survived, I would work the rest of my life to discover the origin and original cause of war so that we could banish it. As shown in the following chapters I have discovered these, greatly by discovering and following the course of The Human Experiment.

The other reason is that my *overall* purpose in writing the book is the result of our growing awareness that we humans are on a self-destructive course, and that, as shown in this book, we now have enough information showing us how we got ourselves onto it, to see how to get ourselves off of it. Following the course of the Human Experiment has been central to gaining that information too. All of this new information is presented clearly in Part II - Our New Human Story.

At the same time, I have wanted to show through my personal experience the insanity and cruelty of war, to help us be sufficiently motivated to banish it. Therefore this experience is shown in Part I - World War II.

Explanatory Note:

Kurt Vonnegut died some time ago, so how has he been able to endorse this present book? A friend of my older brother, Kurt was a frequent guest in our childhood home. Later, when we both lived in New York, Kurt and I got to know one another more directly and he became a lifelong friend. The manuscript of this book was written over a very long period of time, and during that writing Kurt did me the kind favor of critiquing it. When it was completed I asked him if he would endorse it, which he did. I am certain that he would desire me to include his endorsement now that it is finally a book being published, because it continues to include all of the ideas so important to both of us.

James M. Jeffrey

April, 2014

Table of Contents

PART I
World War II

The Hillside

It was dawn of the frozen morning of January 2, 1945 in a snow-covered forest in the northern region of Alsace, France. I was lying asleep on the hard ground, fully dressed in several layers of U.S. Army winter uniform. The clothing had kept me from freezing during the night, but as the daylight woke me I found that my muscles and joints were stiff and sore from the cold. As my eyes blinked open I wondered where I was, and why. Raising myself on one elbow I looked around, saw five other huddled forms, and then I remembered.

From dawn of New Year's Day our American force had been fighting through a seemingly endless forest in a furious battle with an attacking German force, and by sundown we were exhausted. Seeking a place to spend the night, six of us young PFCs (Privates First Class) in an "A" Company light machine gun squad had climbed part way up a high, steep hill to a clearing in the trees. On reaching it we found a shallow depression which overlooked the road below us. From the size and shape of the depression we judged that a small concrete bunker had been built there by the French to control the road, but for some reason had been removed by the occupying Germans.

That same evening "B" Company had taken positions on a hillside across the road and to the right of us, and as the morning mists lifted we looked over to see what they were doing. They were some distance away, but we could see them moving among the pine trees in their overcoats, batting their arms to get warm. Then we suddenly realized; overcoats! We don't wear overcoats! They were enemy soldiers. We had lost contact with our own "A" Company, and now "B" Company was gone; we were alone in enemy territory, and probably surrounded.

The events which led directly to our plight had begun two and a half weeks before during what became known, because of the shape of the battleground, as "The Battle of the Bulge." It was fought during the coldest, snowiest winter "in memory" and involved over a million men: 500 thousand Germans, 600 thousand Americans, 55 thousand British, plus contingents of Belgians, Canadians, and French.

By the fall of 1944 Hitler's generals had seen that defeat for Germany was inevitable, and some of them said the Western Front should be allowed to collapse and all of Germany's force be used to hold back the Russians; they thought it better that Germany be overrun by the Western Allies than by the Reds. But Hitler, the insane, murderous, fascist dictator, believed himself to be infallible, and that if he and his Third Reich were to fall it would be because the Germans were unworthy of his leadership; he felt that if this proved to be the case, there was no reason why Germany and Germans deserved to survive him. Against the advice of his generals he personally planned what he thought to be a master stroke.

By a surprise attack they would break through the weak Allied sector in the Ardennes Forest in Luxembourg, then race across Belgium and capture the great port of Antwerp, thereby splitting the Allied armies in two. While the Allies reeled back, the Germans could race back across Germany and defeat the Russian offensive that was expected to begin early in 1945. The German generals said the plan could not succeed, but Hitler overrode them. Using its extraordinary organizational skills the German high command scraped together most of their strategic reserves, some taken from the Eastern Front, to form a formidable force of 38 divisions, including two Panzer (armored) armies, the Fifth and Sixth. They waited for a period of bad weather to come in and ground the Allied air forces, and early on the morning of December 16, 1944, they struck.

Under cover of heavy fog, the 38 German divisions advanced along a 50-mile front. Armored units overran several First Army positions, and by Christmas Day had driven 60 miles, almost to the Meuse River. On the way they had surrounded the town of Bastogne in the southern Ardennes; ordered to surrender, the Commander of the 101st Airborne Division at Bastogne gave his subsequently famous reply: "Nuts!" Heavy fog continued to prevent Allied planes from giving much-needed air support to Allied forces fighting on the ground. In spite of having no winter clothing or boots, being short of ammunition, food, and medical supplies, no artillery or tanks, freezing in their foxholes, being horrendously bombarded by artillery with heavy losses, the 101st held out from December 20 to 26 and not only slowed the German Fifth Panzer Army, but stopped them, because it kept them from capturing American fuel dumps on which they had counted.

To the great joy of the Allied ground forces, on December 26 the sky cleared permitting Allied fighter–bombers to range everywhere over the battlefield and give them support, including dropping supplies to Bastogne. Several allied armored divisions crashed into the Germans' northern flank, and Third Army units fought their way through the Germans' southern flank to the encircled troops at Bastogne. The Allied newspapers reported that The Battle of the Bulge was over, but it was not, because at this point two terrible mistakes were made, one on each side.

On the German side, the General Staff wanted to order a fast retreat, but Hitler insisted that their troops try to hold every inch of frozen ground. On the Allied side, Patton wanted his Third Army to drive northward and cut off the German troops still in the bulge, but Eisenhower refused him and ordered the troops to push the enemy back inch by inch through the frozen fields and forests.

The hardships of the men fighting on both sides were horrible. A veteran later said the feeling was that if you were lucky you would be hit in the leg, because if you were hit in the arm you would be bandaged and sent right back into the line; but if you were really lucky you would be hit in the head, because in those terrible conditions it was easier to die than it was to live.

The casualties were enormous. By mid-January the Germans had been pushed back to where they had started from, and had lost 100 thousand men killed or wounded, 110 thousand men taken prisoner, some 800 tanks, and most of their remaining aircraft.

The Allies had lost 16 thousand men killed, 60 thousand wounded, over 23 thousand taken prisoner, some 800 tanks, and many aircraft. When the Allies reached the line from which they had been pushed back no big announcement was made, and they just kept going on into Germany. It took three years to find the remains of all of the men who had died in those bitter conditions.

As stated, the Third Army had moved northward to relieve Bastogne and help stop the enemy advance. To fill the gap left by the Third Army, units from the Seventh Army, including my armored infantry battalion, had raced northward; this meant that our defenses there were spread thin. When Field Marshal von Rundstedt saw that his attack in the north had failed, and that our defenses south of the Bulge had been weakened, he pulled a large force out of the battle and sent them against us in a final effort to break through. His plan was that even if this new attack did not break through our Seventh Army it might cause the Third Army to return south, which would relieve pressure on the German units deep in the Bulge as they fought to withdraw without being cut off and trapped... which they could have been if Eisenhower had permitted it.

The German counterattack hit us before dawn on January 1, 1945, and all that day they had been fighting to break through us and we had been fighting to hold them back.

My unit was the 62 nd Armored Infantry Battalion of the 14th Armored Division, and formed part of the Seventh Army. Infantry, tanks, and artillery need each other for protection, so our Division included three battalions of each. On August 15, 1944 the US Seventh Army and the French First Army had made an amphibious landing near Cannes in southern France, and from there they had fought northward up the Rhone Valley. The US Third Army had come from the north, and the two Armies met near Dijon on September 15.

After the amphibious landing near Cannes the 14th Armored Division landed in the nearby port city of Marseille, and became part of the Seventh Army. Marseilles had already been occupied by the Allies, so our troopship was able to tie up at a pier. With our duffel bags over our shoulders we walked down the gang-planks and were trucked to a large, muddy field outside of the city where we set up our two-man tents and stayed for a week.

We were allowed to go into town, and this was an exciting adventure; there were soldiers and sailors everywhere, wearing the uniforms of many countries. One wet night some of us went into a place where we had been told that naked ladies put on a show in order to entice customers to partake of their trade. The show was pathetic and I felt sorry for the ladies, especially since I knew that people had to do whatever they could to get money for food. Just as the performance ended the MPs came in the front door and we went out the back door.

On another night I was passing the entrance to an alley and heard someone screaming, so I walked in to see what was happening. There were three G.I.s (U.S. soldiers) holding a screaming, writhing fourth one down on the wet cobblestones. I asked one of the holders what was wrong, and he turned to me and said that the guy was their buddy and they could take care of him. He said that the screaming one had seen too much combat. As he talked we were looking into each other's faces, and what I saw deep in his eyes really scared me: the horrors of war, the shadows of death, heavy tiredness and sadness, and pity for me the young, green recruit.

Our Division was split into several units, and from Marseille my unit went northward by rail to Epinal. The Germans had taken all of the good rolling stock so we were riding in WW I boxcars. The train kept stopping, waiting, and starting, and the trip lasted three days. We ran out of food so I hopped out and pulled a rutabaga out of a field and ate it raw. It might have been alright by itself, but I drank some canned grapefruit juice with it and was really sick for about three days.

In Epinal we got into our vehicles, called "halftracks," which had wheels in front and tracks behind so that they could negotiate rough terrain and keep up with the tanks and self-propelled field artillery. The halftracks had a closed cab in front and an open rectangular metal box in the rear with a metal bench seat along each side. The driver and the two sergeants sat in the front and the other nine of us in our squad sat facing each other on the two benches with our legs squeezed between each other's. It was a rough ride, but we were young. A 50 caliber machine gun was mounted above the cab, and our three 30 caliber light machine guns were mounted on the armored sides in the back.

My Company "A" was made part of a Combat Command which included tanks, and we rolled eastward along a road in a long column. I cannot remember whether it was when we were going through Epinal or through some other town that the people lined the main street and cheered us and handed us gifts of fruit, wine, and flowers.

We kept rolling eastward, and after a while a German reconnaissance plane zoomed very low directly along our column. Shortly afterward an artillery shell burst to the right of us about 100 yards away, so the column halted and we jumped out of our halftrack and into a ditch by the side of the road. A second shell burst nearer, and then a third nearer still. I suddenly realized that the bursts were in a direct line toward me, and that if there were a fourth one it would land right where I was. In the States I had thought about the possibility of being wounded, but this was the first time I realized that I could get blown into pieces. I tried to crawl completely into my helmet, and just then a shell zipped right over me and exploded on the other side of the road. No men or vehicles had been hit, so we rolled on unhurt. But I had a new and sinking feeling about the future.

I do not remember where it was that I first saw a dead German soldier. He was lying on his face on the ground and his skin was gray like his uniform. I was very shocked and felt a sickness in my stomach because I realized that he was a *person*. He was middle sized and looked just like us, except that he had on a different uniform and he was really, really dead, because somebody like us had killed him. I thought that the war was almost unbelievably horrible and inhuman.

We soon learned that our first mission was to fight our way through the Vosges Mountains, which we did. The road climbed up and down with many switchbacks across valleys, and these were the Germans' favorite places to fell trees and build roadblocks. At one point our side of a wide switchback in the road was blocked and enemy soldiers were firing on us from the other side of the valley. Our tanks were equipped to move the block, but would not have been able to proceed past it for fear of the deadly German anti-tank bazookas. The tanks fired cannon shell after shell at the enemy, but they were too well dug in for direct fire to hit them. We infantrymen could have circled around behind them, but we had a better idea. Our mortar squad came up and lobbed two shells up into the air so that they fell down into the foxholes. I was astounded to see that immediately some 30 soldiers leaped up with their hands raised high. They were escorted back as prisoners, a bulldozer tank cleared the way, and we moved on to the next roadblock.

After several days we emerged from the mountains onto the Plain of Alsace, and after the war I learned that this was the first time in history that an attacking force had been able to pass through the Vosges when they were being defended, as the mountains were a natural fortress. However, as I write this I realize that we were just lucky. At this time the German High Command could not spare even one tank to defend the south of France. They were all needed in the north and on the Russian Front. In the mountains even one Tiger tank could have given us a very hard time. But it was good training for us green troops, and it was scary, because we thought there was a tank with the dreaded 88 millimeter cannon waiting around every turn in the road.

On reaching the Alsatian Plain we continued east to Colmar where we turned north and rolled along between the mountain range and the Rhine River. Sometimes we would fire our guns from the moving vehicle, aiming at possible danger spots in towns or in the countryside; other times the column would halt and the officers would yell, "Dismount!" We would then leap out with our rifles and carbines, two of the 30 caliber machine guns, the bazooka, hand grenades, and ammunition, and become non-armored infantry, and the officers would yell, "Get those vehicles to the rear!" At these moments I wished I had been a driver, though there were other moments when I was glad I was not.

In one town where we dismounted I was walking along the side of a building when I heard a shot and felt something hit my pant leg. I thought, "Hotdog, I've been hit, and it doesn't even hurt, and I'll be sent back!" But the bullet had hit the wall and a piece of something had hit my pant leg without even tearing it. What a disappointment. And I couldn't find the sniper.

When we reached the town of Barr a terrible mistake was made, because it was reported that it was unoccupied. Instead of having us dismount and go in first as infantry, they let some tanks lead. When we went through the town in our halftracks it was a sight I shall never forget. What had been four or more moving Sherman tanks were now stationary, burning hulks, with blackened corpses halfway out of the turrets, their skulls and wrist bones blanched ghastly white. The enemy soldiers had hidden in buildings on both sides of the narrow main street and had waited until the tanks had entered the town; then they had all fired their bazookas at once at short range. The missiles were designed to stick to the side of a tank and burn through setting the tank on fire inside and burning to death the entire crew. All of the enemy soldiers escaped.

Once when the column halted on an exposed road our First Lieutenant walked past our halftrack and we asked him why he had a strap fastened from his helmet to his jacket. He said, "Because when I have to run like this, and my helmet falls off like this, I won't have to stop and pick it up." Five minutes later, a sniper's bullet hit him in the testicles, and we heard that his scrotum swelled like a balloon. We really liked him and were very worried about his wound, but we heard later that he was going to be OK.

Another time we had to dismount on a completely dark night and hold a line across a large open area. It was muddy and there were puddles of ice cold water everywhere. Harold and I set up the machine gun and lay down beside it. I said that I was not going to take cover in a puddle no matter what. Then enemy machine guns began to fire, and tracer bullets were making bright red and orange lines as they flew overhead. We were irresistibly drawn up off the ground to watch them when somebody yelled, "Stay down! Grazing fire!", and I rolled into the nearest puddle. It was a German trick; they fired the tracers high to make us rise up, and fired regular bullets low to the ground to hit us. Then we heard tanks moving. They always made a lot of noise, with their tracks clanking, and their engines roaring as they constantly shifted gears. But for some reason you could never tell by the sounds in which direction they were moving, whether they were coming at you or going away, which was scary. Then it sounded like the screaming of all of the demons of hell as the Germans fired a fusillade of rockets from the Wofflewerbers, or whatever they called them. We called them Screaming Meemmies. Nothing else happened where we were, and we left just before dawn. A crazy night.

We were cold, hungry, tired, wet, and miserable most of the time. In each small box of "K" Rations was a tiny cardboard carton containing two cigarettes. When it was raining I would throw away one cigarette and smoke the other one inside the carton to keep it dry. At one point we were lucky to be issued the new snow boots and sleeping bags. The waterproof boots kept our feet dry and warm, which was like a miracle.

We also got waterproof mittens and wool gloves to fit inside them. The sleeping bags were thin, but as we took off only our boots before crawling into them we kept warm. However, just when you would get the bag warmed up and fall asleep somebody would shake you to get up and put on your cold boots for guard duty.

We kept moving northward until one day Lester, who had the best eyesight, said, "Oh my God!" What he had seen were the "dragon's teeth," the concrete anti-tank spikes running row on row in front of the German defenses called the "Siegfried Line." We dismounted and walked toward them, why I shall never know, until suddenly the ground all around us began to erupt with mortar shell explosions. We had seen trenches along the road, so we raced for them and dived in, all except my best friend, who had had both his legs blown off and was killed instantly. We stayed in the trenches all day and watched huge flights of our bombers passing high above us toward Germany. After dark we walked back to our vehicles and bedded down. We were high on a hill, and again I saw a sight I shall never forget: the eerie red glow of three towns burning in the distance. It was deathly quiet and totally surrealistic. The next morning a company of infantry occupied the area and began digging in. They were green, and some were locating their foxholes under trees, so we warned them not to because of shells bursting in the branches, which we called "tree bursts." As we climbed into our halftrack and sat on the benches facing each other, and Tommy was not there any more, I will not attempt to describe my thoughts and feelings, and will say only that I was in shock and very sorry that he got hit and was dead.

At this point our Battalion was in the northernmost region of Alsace, and it was December 30, 1944. We knew what had happened in the Bulge and were expecting a German assault, so "A" and "B" Companies moved to a defensive position in a snow-covered forest. Although the ground was frozen we were able to break through the crust, dig two-man foxholes, and cover them with logs and earth. My "A" Company machine gun squad was two men under strength because of one dead and one sick, and the rifle, mortar, and machine gun squads in other companies of the battalion were also under strength because of men killed, or wounded, or sick, or frostbitten.

New Year's Eve we were on special alert, as there had been enemy forces attacking on our flanks and an attack was expected at any time on our own position. Covered in snow on this moonlit night, the terrain was thought to be in our favor, as we could observe without being seen. Yet at 3:00 AM on New Year's Day a signal flare was tripped in "A" Company's sector at the barbed wire, and its light revealed an enemy combat patrol, clad in white, which had advanced to within 50 yards without being seen. We fired on the patrol and called on our self-propelled artillery, which was behind us, to fire forward of our position. After the barrage our investigating patrol went out and had just returned when a terrific enemy artillery barrage was brought to bear on our position. Fortunately our well-roofed foxholes prevented us from having casualties, but the barrage was followed by the advance of enemy tanks and infantry. Having no tanks nearby we withdrew and called our artillery to fire on them. This caused them to withdraw, so we counter-attacked. We fired at anything we saw in front of us that was not a tree. Then we got too far away from our defensive position and pulled back.

This see-sawing back and forth continued all through the day and we became greatly fatigued. The various units in our force intermingled and lines of communication broke down. How many men on either side were being wounded or killed was unknown to us.

During one of the times when we were pulling back, a man I did not know sat on a log and said he didn't care what happened, he wasn't moving. Just then one of the extremely rapid firing German automatic pistols, a "burp gun" as we called it because of the sound it made, was fired nearby. "Br-r-r-r-r-r-rp!!!" The man sprang from the log and said, "Let's go!" As we had been ordered to withdraw to our defense line we did so and held it.

Another incident wired permanently into my memory is that when I first scrambled out of my foxhole to attack I grabbed two cardboard tubes containing hand grenades, and while walking along at a swift pace pulled one tube apart too fast. It popped open, the grenade flew out and fell on the ground, and to my horror I saw that the pin had come almost all the way out of it. My hands were numb with cold but I managed to pick up the grenade, push the pin back in, and stow the grenade in my field jacket pocket, all while walking quickly along, holding a 30 caliber machine gun on one shoulder, with my carbine slung over my other shoulder. I always wondered what I would have done if the grenade's pin had come all the way out, as there were men all around me.

At one point in the battle a member of my squad fired our bazooka and broke the track mechanism of a German tank. However, its guns kept us pinned down while another tank came and dragged it away. We thought it was a very brave act by the tankers, but were disappointed at not having been able to capture the tank. Nevertheless, it is a frightening feeling to be pinned down by a rapidly firing tank cannon, not knowing if another tank will suddenly come clanking and roaring right at you, and I was quite relieved when the iron monsters went away.

By late afternoon units on our right and left flanks had been forced to give ground to the enemy, so to prevent our being encircled the order was given to withdraw to secondary defense positions. As we walked along a narrow forest road our column was suddenly strafed and bombed by enemy planes, but the bombs went wide of the target and as we leaped off the road the machine gun bullets missed us by a few feet. We were surprised that the Luftwaffe still had pilots and planes to send against us. By this time it was evening and everyone was exhausted. It had been a terrible, chaotic day and, as was usual during a fight, it seemed that no one knew what was going on, or who was winning or losing, or where he ought to be.

As previously noted, six of our machine gun squad had managed to stick together; we were all about 19 years of age, and all Pfcs. As it grew dark we climbed a hill, found the afore-mentioned depression, and took cover in it for the night. We ate some "K" Rations and went to sleep, but around midnight were awakened by the noise of moving tanks and firing. From then on the night passed very slowly and was a frightening time, with the sounds of unseen tanks coming and going, and the darkness being pierced periodically by the bright red lines of tracer bullets sailing around. Then down on the road below us there was the sound of running feet, followed by shots, and then right below us someone moaning. We could see nothing, and had no idea of who was where or why. It seemed the moaning would go on forever, but finally it stopped and I went to sleep again.

As stated, at daylight on January 2nd I awoke with the others and found that the hillside across the road to the right of us had been vacated by "B" Company and was now occupied by the large force of enemy soldiers. We kept down out of sight, and could do nothing but watch and wait. After a while all of the overcoated figures climbed down the hillside to the road below us and walked along it in our direction. There were many of them, and we did not know how many more of them might be nearby, so we were very relieved as we thought they were leaving the area. To our great alarm however, as they arrived below us they began climbing the hillside directly across the road from us.

There was room on the side of the depression for only two persons, so Louis and I lay on our stomachs peering over the edge while the other four kept out of sight at our feet. It was clear that the enemy was unaware of our presence. They were laughing and calling to each other as they climbed up the wooded hillside, sometimes slipping on the snow. Louis and I looked at each other, and asked each other what in the hell we had better do. We did not know why they were climbing the hillside, but we figured that if they got to a point higher than our hiding place they would see us. Having nothing to hide behind we would have to engage in a fire-fight with a greatly larger force, or surrender. The former course was suicidal and we thought the latter might be too, as we had recently heard of the atrocity committed up north, where Nazi SS troops had massacred over one hundred American prisoners in an open field.

We assumed that our forces had pulled back and that we were alone in enemy territory. We had planned to wait until nightfall, and then try to slip through and rejoin our Company, but this new development destroyed our plan. Louis and I selected a certain place on the hillside being climbed by the enemy soldiers and agreed that if they climbed that high we would open fire. He would take the left, and I the right. I trained the sights of my carbine on the man highest up on the right, tightened my finger slightly on the trigger, and waited.

As he climbed I thought to myself, "My God, I am about to kill a man! How did I get into this?" It was not that killing and death were new to me. We had been in fire-fights, and had seen many horrible sights: close friends wounded or killed; soldiers on both sides bloody, maimed, dead, bloated; the blackened corpses halfway out of the turrets of the burning Sherman tanks; horses and cows with parts of their legs blown off, screaming, stumbling backwards with wildly terrified eyes.

I had fired at many targets, from our moving halftrack and from on foot. But I had never known for sure whether or not I had hit or killed anyone. It had always been so chaotic during a fight, with so much running around, and terrible noise and explosions, and smoke, and stench, that it was impossible to know exactly what was happening... and we always left immediately afterward, going on to the next fight and leaving someone else to count and dispose of the corpses.

This was very different. Now, I was looking directly at another person, who was laughing and full of life, and I was quietly, consciously, preparing to kill him in cold blood... to shoot him in the back without warning. But if I did not kill him, he was going to kill me. "Anyway," I thought, "I am *supposed* to kill him. I am a soldier, and he is the enemy, and I was put in this uniform, and given this gun, and trained to kill him. This is what they sent me across the ocean to do.

But I don't even *know* this guy. Who the hell had the right to put me in this position? Why did I let them put me in this position? Because I was ignorant and naive. But that was then and this is now. You can't let Louis and the other guys down. You can't be a yellow coward. OK. Do it. But on one condition. If you get out of this, if you get home again, you will work the rest of your life to make sure that no one will ever be able to put you or anyone else in this position again. Now squeeze!"

I squeezed the trigger and through my sights saw a figure slump. I squeezed again and he fell to the ground and slid a short way down the hillside, leaving a dark track in the snow. Louis had fired at the same moment, and I saw a figure to the left fall and slide a way down. Louis had to hit them only once with his M-1 rifle, but with my carbine I had to hit them twice. It evened out though, as my clip held more bullets than his. We both kept firing as fast as we could move our sights from one figure to another, and the other guys handed us new clips of ammunition as we needed them.

As Louis and I fired, I had a feeling of great excitement and elation. It was not because I was killing persons, because once I had begun firing they were no longer persons, but dangerous, feared, highly-trained, weapon-using enemies. The excitement and elation came from having made and carried out the decision not to be immobilized, not to be helpless, rather to have had the ability to take our lives into our own hands, and to fight for our survival, and to be doing it effectively, even though we thought we would probably not live to tell the tale. Put somewhat differently, once it was clear that someone was going to do it to someone, I was very glad that we were doing it to them rather than they doing it to us.

As we kept firing, figures kept falling, and sliding, until there was no more movement on the hillside. Most of them had not been hit, as they had taken cover behind trees and rocks. We stopped firing and I laid down my carbine and put the machine gun up on the edge. If anyone moved I put a burst of fire at him.

As we were wondering what could happen next there was a terrific explosion on the hill occupied by the enemy, followed by two more such explosions. Suddenly the enemy soldiers began moving and I fired a burst with the machine gun. At that moment, to our great amazement voices from down the road to the left shouted, "Cease firing, cease firing!" and all of the enemy soldiers on the hillside stood up with their hands raised above their heads. We thought it had to be a trick, but they had seen something we could not yet see. After a few seconds we heard the roar of engines and the clanking of tracks, and around the bend in the road came a most welcome and beautiful sight... two Sherman tanks, followed by men wearing field jackets and carrying rifles. The explosions on the enemy's hill had been from shells fired by the tanks' cannons. The Captain of "A" Company had made it back to our line and had found about 10 men, including the battalion cooks, and had obtained two tanks from down the line to relieve us. Caught in a crossfire between our two forces the German force had no choice but to surrender or be annihilated. I felt guilty that I had fired a burst before I knew they were trying to surrender, and hoped I had not hit anyone, though I thought I had.

We learned later that all along our battalion defense line there had been heavy fighting through the previous day and night and that morning. About 20 "A" Company men had held out in a shallow trench near us. A lieutenant had tried to find an escape route but was wounded by rifle fire and fell to the ground. A sergeant ran out from the trench, reached the wounded man, and brought him the several hundred feet back to the trench, amazingly neither he nor the lieutenant being hit by enemy fire aimed at them. When our tanks arrived, the enemy soldiers who had had these men pinned down were also caught in a crossfire, and surrendered. Infiltrating enemy patrols had forced "B" Company to fall back to new positions during the night, but with the aid of 4.2 mortars they held out. Many of our men were killed, wounded, or missing, but except in one place we had been able to hold the line against a numerically superior force. The men of Headquarters Company and "C" Company had held the town of Bannstein during fierce infantry fighting, but were forced to abandon it when German tanks came and began smashing down the buildings in which they had taken cover. A section of Headquarters Company was surrounded and cut off completely, and the fate of the men was still unknown.

No account of combat should ignore the role of the Medic, the Aid Man with each platoon who went under as much fire as anyone, but without a weapon to protect himself. When someone was hit he or someone near would yell, "Medic!", and would expect him to come running over and staunch the flow of blood, stick the morphine needle in to numb the pain, sprinkle the sulfa powder on the wound, splint the broken bone, or whatever. I did not realize it until I was writing this, but the fact that we *expected* him to come, regardless of the danger to which he had to expose himself, was the highest tribute we could give him. Too many of these unprotected heroes died in their attempts to save others.

The Valley

Shortly after the enemy attack had been launched we had been told that a regiment of infantry was to arrive soon to relieve our battalion, and they happened to arrive shortly after the German force surrendered. They were excited to see so many prisoners, but they had not yet been in combat and to their eyes the scene of dead and wounded men was horrible. But those of us who had just come through two hellish days of fighting for survival could see only that one more bad time was over, that we were still alive, that we were finally being relieved, that we might get to go someplace where we could sleep, eat, and get dry and warm, and that these poor bastards relieving us hadn't yet learned how to take care of themselves and were going to get the shit kicked out of them by the Krauts, but that there was nothing we could do about it. (About half of our words were very obscene but very satisfying.) We learned later that this is exactly what happened to them.

Leaving the infantry regiment to replace us we withdrew to the village of Ingwiller, where we had outpost duty for a week and our dream of eating, sleeping, and keeping warm came true. We had hot meals at the battalion kitchen, and stayed in a big, old, wonderful farmhouse owned by a wonderful farmer named Irgen. He was about 50 years old, with sparkling eyes, red cheeks, and tousled red hair. He was full of life, quite jovial, and seemed really to like us and to consider us his boys. He gave us delicious apples, cider, and schnapps. He spoke English fairly well with a German accent, and we asked him if he thought of himself as being German or French. He replied, "I am Alsatian. When the French come, I speak French. When the Germans come, I speak German. If the Chinese come tomorrow, I will speak Chinese. But I am Alsatian." As I write this I realize that he was too much a gentleman to add that with our coming, he was speaking English. Irgen was what the harassed people of war-torn Europe had to be... a survivor.

I was 5' 8 1/2" in tall and weighed 140 pounds; Irgen was about my height, but heavier, and quite strong and nimble. He led six of us up two flights of stairs to a big loft under the roof where apples and other fruits were drying, and gave us down comforters; two of us slept on a bed and four of us on the floor on straw mattresses. Each morning while we were getting up Irgen would come up and make everyone take a drink of schnapps, insisting that it was good for us. It was strong stuff, and after the fifth day Louis said he couldn't take it any more and hid under the bed. When Irgen came up he poured the five of us glasses of schnapps, and then wandered around the room saying, "Ver's der Looie? Ver's der Looie?" Louis was about my size, with red hair and gold wire-rimmed spectacles. Irgen found him under the bed, pulled him out by one leg, and made him drink his share while sitting on the floor in his long johns.

On January 12, though numerically far under strength, the Battalion was again committed to combat. It was the first time that the units of the Battalion had all been together, and the first time that our Company had been under the command of our Battalion Commander. We thought that all of us being under our own officer would be better for us than when we were split into units under other officers.

Before dawn we climbed into our halftracks and moved toward the enemy line. As the daylight came we dismounted and found ourselves in the midst of a great expanse of rolling farmland covered in snow; on orders, we spread out across an open field behind a wide crest. The Captain of "A" Company was leading the advance, and on his signal we moved up toward the crest. Upon reaching it, he called out to us to halt and dig in. The commanding officer of the battalion, a Lieutenant Colonel, had stayed behind, but at this point he came running out to us and I heard him say to the Captain, "Why'd you stop?!" The Captain then called out, "OK men, let's go!" The Lieutenant Colonel then ran back to where he had come from.

Ahead of and horizontal to us lay a valley. The land went in a long slope downward, at the bottom of which it rose again in a long slope upward. We left the crest and started down the open slope in a spread-out formation about 200 yards wide. I was in the front of the formation, near the Captain, and when we had descended about 50 yards we heard an ear-splitting roar behind us. We looked back and saw the entire length of the crest disappear in a cloud of dirt and smoke. I was so shocked that for a second I could neither understand nor believe what had happened. Then I had the terrifying realization that we were caught in a trap, and that the explosions behind us were the first volley of the most horrendous and concentrated German artillery barrage that I had ever seen. The Captain yelled, "All right men, no one's been hurt yet! Keep going!" We kept going, but the line of explosions swept down the slope in a moving barrage right onto our entire formation. The last command I heard was the Captain yelling, "Get those automatic weapons going!"

Harold, who two days before had rejoined the squad, immediately threw the machine gun tripod to the ground and took the prone position behind it. As Peter came running over with a cannister of ammunition I set the machine gun into the tripod, then fed the belt of ammunition into the breach as Harold worked the cocking mechanism and began firing. I had no idea what he was firing at, and never found out, because after a few seconds he was hit in the throat by a piece of shrapnel and crawled backward away from the gun. In a state of shock, and not knowing what else to do, I crawled behind the gun and began firing at what appeared to be something or someone in the distance, but there was so much smoke and flying debris I could not be sure. A few seconds later there was a terrific explosion to my immediate right; my steel helmet was blown off my head, my wire-rimmed spectacles were blown off my face, and there was a loud ringing in my ears and the taste of blood in my mouth. It felt as if someone had hit me a stunning blow square in the face with a big, hard boxing glove. After the ringing toned down a bit I found that my right eye was closed and my right hand would not work; but I figured I would survive. I remember thinking that after what I had done to the enemy, I could not complain that he did it back to me.

But just then another shell burst immediately to my left and shattered both bones in my left leg below my knee and above my boot. My leg flipped around in the air for a few seconds, bending at the break. I remember being angry because it seemed to me that having been hit once was enough, and that hitting me twice was going too far. In retrospect, I remember that I was hitting them twice with my carbine, so now I know how they too must have felt. From the extreme way my leg had been flopping around below the break I assumed the artery had been severed, and that I would bleed to death. Using my left hand, I pulled out my boot lace and tried to use it as a tourniquet, but I was wearing heavy clothing and was not able to twist it tight. I pulled the hood of my field jacket over my head and lay back in the snow. Lying there I remembered that we were instructed to destroy our guns to keep the enemy from using them against us. The only thing I could think of to do in my condition was to try to hold back the trigger of the machine gun and burn out the barrel. I began firing, but suddenly a bullet just missed the top of my skull and snapped the hood of my field jacket back off my head, and I got the message. I stopped firing, pulled out my handkerchief and waved it back and forth a few times in a token of surrender.

By this time I was quite tired and weak; I must have felt totally helpless, abandoned, alone, and terrified, because I remember calling out for my Mother. Finally I assumed I was going to die, so I gave up and lay back in the snow, feeling somewhat ashamed at having waved the surrender flag. At that moment I remembered the American volunteer in Hemingway's story about the Spanish war, "For Whom the Bell Tolls." At the end of the story he too had his leg broken by enemy fire, and lying on the ground behind his machine gun he could feel his heart beating against the pine needles as he waited for the moment when he was to die. I thought, "Now it's my turn.", and closed my eye and went to sleep.

POW

The sound of shots being fired wakened me. I was very surprised that I was still alive. It occurred to me that the Germans might be going around the battlefield shooting men they thought to be near death, so I decided to look very much alive. I raised up on my left elbow and through my left eye saw a German soldier with a rifle. He came over and beckoned to me saying, "Kommen Sie! Kommen Sie!" I pointed to my left leg and said, "Kaput! Kaput!" He became quite excited, gestured with his rifle and repeated, "Kommen Sie! Kommen Sie!"

At this point out of the corner of my eye I saw some men coming with their arms raised above their heads. I did not know if they had been wounded. I called to them and they came over, and with the consent of our captors they picked me up. I think there were four of them, and two of them made a seat by interlocking their arms and began carrying me to the enemy line. For a while they took turns carrying me in this way but it was very difficult for them and for me; my left leg kept swinging back and forth at the break in the bones, causing me to feel extreme pain, and I kept reaching down with my left hand to hold onto the top of my boot in an effort to keep the bones from grating against each other. This threw my carriers off balance, so finally one man took me on his back with his arms under my thighs; he was a good friend, named Al, from another platoon in "A" Company. Riding on his back I was able to hold onto him with my right arm around his neck and hold onto my boot with my left hand, but it continued to swing and was quite painful. Blood was dripping from my face onto Al's head, and I remember apologizing to him for this. He said not to worry about it. Although I was unaware of it, while he was carrying me he was suffering from a wound in his heel. After what seemed a very long time we reached the enemy line and came to a huge concrete fortification; there Al walked along a narrow plank which crossed a deep trench, and we entered through an open doorway of steel. Once inside Al put me down on the floor against a wall and I passed out.

The following is from the Battalion History: "The attack was begun across an open field in battalion strength. The Battalion was in the attack that was to have taken ground west of Hatten and Rittershoffen and suffered severely under the mortar and artillery barrages the Germans had in waiting, and released once the last man was exposed. The day was so bitterly cold that men froze to the ground where they fell, so there were few men to make the escape when orders were given to withdraw; it was here that "A" Company suffered the loss of the company commander, Captain Iannella, the man who had led the company through so much of its training and all of its combat. His loss was deeply felt, and for months was the cause of much speculation; no one knew (whether) he had been taken prisoner, wounded, or killed."

When the barrage hit us I was too busy setting up, loading, and subsequently firing the machine gun to see what was going on around me, except that the whole place was exploding, and that Harold had been hit. However, four months later the Captain and I were in the same Army Hospital in Chicago and he told me that he had been wounded and captured, and that he had seen several men cut and blown to pieces. He saw a sergeant next to him, his close friend, using both hands to try to push his intestines back where they had been before a fragment ripped his stomach open, a look of stunned bewilderment on his face before he fell dead. Then the Captain was hit and lost consciousness. In my own squad I know of four who were killed, including my valiant friend Louis; some were wounded, and some were made prisoner, and one that I know of managed to survive the barrage and make it back to our lines.

While I was unconscious on the floor of the pillbox someone bandaged my wounds and put a splint on my leg. At some point I heard someone yell, "Amerikanishe Panzer kommen!" I thought, "Great!" But no one appeared to liberate me, so I drifted off again. Later, I was awakened by a German soldier who gave me a canteen cup of a warm, sweet liquid to drink. Then I was carried on a stretcher and put into the back of a vehicle along with other wounded men. The vehicle had a canvas top, and I could feel the weight of a man pressing down on me who was lying on the canvas. It grew dark as we bumped along, and I kept passing out and in.

After a while we crossed the Rhine River (though I was not aware of it) and finally arrived at an Army Hospital in Mannheim, Germany, where I was carried in on my stretcher to a very large room on the ground floor, and was put down among a sea of other wounded men on stretchers, many more German soldiers than American. It was a scene from Hell... men lying or sitting all over the place, in all stages of agony, injury, and dismemberment, some moaning, some crying out for help; red blood seeping through white bandages, and orderlies and nurses hurrying among us, trying to attend to those most in need; many of us waiting for surgery. I waited for a long time, passing out and in, and then it was my turn.

I was taken to an operating room, and remember feeling quite relieved because the doctors and nurses there seemed friendly and caring during the few moments before I was put to sleep. They must have been these, and also competent, because I received excellent medical treatment, including having all of my wounds treated, and (perhaps) having the pieces of my leg bones put back together, and my leg put in a cast. When I woke up the next morning I was in a real bed. I do not remember the room, but I think I was in clean white sheets with my head on a clean white pillow. The first thing I thought was, "Have I still got my leg?" I was surprised and extremely happy to discover that it was still there, because I had expected that my leg would be cut off. It was in a cast, my right hand was bandaged and splinted, and my head, right arm and right side were bandaged; my right eye was swollen closed and covered by a bandage, and I assumed it had been permanently blinded. In spite of my physical state, I was quite happy to be alive, and felt extremely fortunate and thankful to have been given such excellent care.

The next day I was carried on a stretcher to a nearby unfinished concrete building and up two flights of stairs to a large unfinished floor open on the sides. There were four other GIs there, all of us on cots. Two of them were P-47 pilots who had had to bail out. One had a broken leg and the face of the other had been burned and he could not see. Administering to us periodically were a young orderly and a nurse who were friendly to us, and another nurse who was not. As she administered the blinded man she said in a bitter voice, "Hah! Drops in your eyes so that you can see to kill more Gemans!" Our building was next to a railroad marshaling yard, which was an exciting place to be, because it was bombed several times by P-47s. As our building shook, we cheered our planes, an act which, understandably, was not appreciated by our German caretakers.

After three days I was moved to Heppenheim and put in a small room on the top floor of a three-story building which had held mental patients before the war, for which reason the windows were barred. There were four of us in the room: Barney was an infantryman about my age who had lost a leg; Joe was the P-47 pilot with the broken leg who had been in the other building with me; Michael was an RAF Lancaster Bomber pilot whose leg also had been broken when he had to bail out. I think that the two pilots were a little older than Barney and me. We were all unable to get out of bed, so all we could do was lie there and think and talk. Joe said he had just missed landing in a place where there were metal stakes in the ground to hold grapevines; a few feet away and he would have been impaled on one. Michael said the most dangerous part of flying a loaded Lancaster Bomber was taking off; if one managed to get it airborne it was a miracle. Barney said he was hit by cannon fire from a German tank, and that after hitting him the tank crewmen leaped out of their tank, ran to him, and apologized.

The most important daily event was the arrival of meals. We were given very little food, and were always hungry. By that time Germany's supplies were quite limited or gone. They innovated where possible, creating "ersatz" whatever. Mainly we had very small pieces of ersatz bread and a cup of what was said to be potato peeling soup, but there were no peelings in it. We were so hungry that at first we agreed not to talk about food, as it only made us feel worse. But each of us was thinking about it all the time anyway, so after a week we changed the rule and after that food was about all that we did talk about. We made lists of every kind of food we could think of, and exchanged menus, and dreamed of what we could have when we got home. A guy from a farm in Nebraska used to come in and visit us, and he would spend hours describing his mother's cellar, in which she had ceiling-high shelves holding long rows of jars of food. "She would put green beans in four one-quart jars, or two two-quart jars, or one one-gallon jar, and peach preserves in....." He kept going through the entire stock of foods, dividing and re-dividing them, never losing his enthusiasm, as though in this way he could actually conjure it all up in our presence. Sometimes it seemed he would never stop, and his talking on and on about drove me nuts. Usually when males get together a main topic of conversation is females; in our condition the subject of sex was of no interest whatever, and was never discussed.

We received minimal medical attention; a man who I think was a French POW came occasionally to change our dressings, but he had very few supplies. I think he used rolls of crepe paper. Every night an old German soldier would come into our room and put a blackout shade over the window to keep our electric ceiling light from showing. Air raid warning sirens would sound day and night. The closer the planes were, the faster the sirens would go. Finally would come the long, steady note of the all clear, but only minutes after it had stopped there would again be the sound of the early warning siren, and the entire sequence would be repeated; fortunately, we were never bombed, although we sometimes heard the sound of bombs exploding and the firing of antiaircraft guns, and sometimes felt the building shudder. Each morning the old soldier would come down the corridor blowing a whistle, and would enter each room and remove the blackout shade. It was snowing and cold outside, and we were cold inside. I learned later that it was the coldest winter in Europe "in memory."

A young GI from Chicago would come into our room sometimes, and upon entering would paraphrase a radio announcer for the Chicago Cubs (or White Sox?), saying, "Hello baseball fans! It's a beautiful day in Chicago, and it's a lousy day in Heppenheim!" Al, who had carried me on his back and saved my life, was there too, and he sometimes came to visit. He reported that a mutual friend, Paul, was also there. Paul had been hit by bazooka fire while leading a patrol on Christmas Day, and taken prisoner. After a month Al came in with the sad news that Paul had died. There were tears in Al's eyes, as he said he had done everything he could to help Paul, but that his wounds had been terrible and at least he was not suffering any more. Shortly after that Harold came in, and except for having a sore and stiff neck he seemed to be doing OK.

About that time two things happened. I thought my right eye had been permanently blinded, but it opened up and was as good as before. Also, two US doctors who had been captured came around from room to room. One was a Major and the other a Captain, and we were very excited to see them, as we thought they would be able to help us a lot medically. However they had almost no medical supplies and so were not able to do much for anyone. The fundamental problem was that we did not have enough to eat, and the doctors could not remedy this. Day by day we were getting thinner, and weaker, and our bad wounds rather than healing were infected and draining. Our condition was so bad that the doctors would operate only when someone was about to die, because if they did operate he would most probably die anyway. A guy next door was screaming and screaming, and finally they took him away and cut off his leg. When he came back he sounded real chipper, and I said I thought he would be OK. Someone said, "He'll be dead before morning." And he was.

I had to lie on my back. I could not turn onto my right side, because pieces of shrapnel had entered the right side of my skull, face, side, and right hand, and another piece had gone through the flesh in my right upper arm, and all five wounds were infected. I could not turn onto my left side, because the leg bones were sticking out of a hole in my cast. The cast was never changed, and as I lost weight, and my leg got thinner, the cast no longer kept my leg extended; it gradually shortened by two and one half inches, forcing the bones to overlap and be pushed outward through the skin on both sides. These areas became infected, so holes were cut in the cast so that dressings could be applied and changed.

After a while bed sores developed on my buttocks, where the bones pressed the skin against the mattress. From somewhere I obtained some kind of padding, and I spent much time shifting it around underneath me to take the pressure off the sore places, as resting on them became increasingly painful. One of the worst parts was getting on a bedpan, both because of my miserable physical condition, and because the German bedpans had sharp edges. I had a metal duck in which to urinate; I was always cold, and as the warm urine filled the duck I kept it between my legs to warm them. The problem was that I would then fall asleep and the urine would become cold, and would spill over me and the bed.

For a pillow I had a small corrugated box, with printing on it which indicated it was from the Red Cross. This was as close as any of us got to receiving any kind of care package.

After three months I was skin and bones, and began hallucinating; I told the other three guys that I knew it was ridiculous, but that I was turning to stone. It started at my feet, and was creeping up my legs; it was really frightening, and I thought that if it kept going it would reach my heart, and it would turn to stone, and I would die. Michael blurted out, in his marvelous English accent, "Quick man! Eat a bit of bread!" I did, and the comic relief caused me to stop hallucinating. I think I would have been dead within a week, but two days later there were several very loud explosions nearby which shook the building and rattled the windows. The noise had been made by the firing of German artillery, and suddenly it stopped. Some GI POWs came into our room and said they were told to carry us down to the basement to get us out of danger. I asked what was going on, and they said they heard that the Americans had crossed the Rhine and were coming. I said to leave me there because I did not want to miss anything.

Liberated

In fact none of the four of us was moved, because just then members of the US Third Infantry Division arrived and liberated us. When they came into our room they almost passed out from the foul odor of infected wounds; we were the first prisoners they had seen, and as they went from room to room they were at once joyous to have saved us, in tears at what we had suffered, and furiously angry at those responsible.

General Devers came through and said, "I want these men in a hospital in Paris by Easter!" (two days away). "But General, sir," said his aides, "everything is moving in this direction now; it is impossible to move them against the flow." Replied the General, "You heard what I said." One of the transport planes would not function properly, so the General told them to use his personal plane. We were in Paris in a hospital by Easter.

Since the time I was hit I had been listed as missing in action and my mother and father and two brothers had been terribly worried. As soon as possible they were notified that I had been found, and this came as a great relief to them. My elder brother was a pilot, and so my family had him to worry about too... plus my cousin who had bailed out of a flaming bomber and was a POW in Germany... and so on. The terrors and suffering of war hit everyone.

The staff of the hospital in Paris brought me the food I had been dreaming of, and I could not eat it. I drank various colors of liquids, swallowed handfuls of multi-colored pills, and was nourished intravenously. The problem was that I had very little flesh on my bones, and my skin was dry and hard and difficult to penetrate with a needle. When they did get a needle in, the vein would slide away under the skin so that several attempts were required to hit it. Penicillin had just been developed, and this is what saved me. The catch was that it had to be administered by needle every three hours. I had so little flesh that the injected area would swell and remain swollen and sore, so they could not stick me twice in the same place.

After two weeks there were no more places to stick me, so I said to the medical officer, "Doc, I know penicillin is the miracle cure, and that it's saving my life, but please take me off of it because I can't stand getting stuck anymore." The doctor looked into my eyes and said, "Son, I have great news for you. They're flying you home." This made me feel extremely happy. He said also that he had been designated to decorate me with the Order of the Purple Heart, and he put the medal beside me in its open box. I was embarrassed and told him I did not want it, as I should have ducked. He said I should accept it. He said, "It's how the people feel." This touched me, so I accepted it.

The Hospital

They strapped me to a stretcher and put me on a four-motored transport plane with other guys strapped to stretchers, and flew us by way of the Azores to New York City. From there they flew us to Army hospitals nearest our homes; for me it was Gardiner General Hospital in Chicago, formerly the Chicago Beach Hotel. I later learned that they had selected the men whom they expected to die, and had flown them back first. I heard that most of the ones on my plane did die, and this shook me. My parents came to visit me, and though they were extremely happy that I was alive, they were extremely shocked to see my condition. To look into my eyes was to see the terror of war and death, and if I were touched anywhere it hurt. However I was given the best of care and was soon on the road to recovery.

As previously noted, the Captain of "A" Company was also there in the hospital. He told me that he had been knocked unconscious by shrapnel entering his right shoulder, and had lain overnight in the snow and suffered frostbite in his hands and feet. He was picked up the next day by German soldiers and taken to an old castle where SS officers interrogated him. He would not give them information other than his name, rank, and serial number, so he was put in a cellar in a dark, cold, damp room. That night he was taken outside and made to dig what he was told would be his own grave, using only his left hand, his right shoulder having been mutilated by the shrapnel. Although quite frightened, he continued to refuse to give information, and next day was sent to a town where he was put into a boxcar jammed with other POWs. There were so many men in the car that they all had to remain standing.

On its way to a POW camp the train was strafed by American planes, and machine gun bullets hit the head of a man standing next to the Captain. The man's head exploded with such force that pieces of his skull entered the Captain's shoulder in the same place where he had been wounded by shrapnel. When the train arrived at the next town he was taken to a hospital and placed on a stretcher on the floor. There were so many wounded that he was ignored for two days and was dying. Finally a young woman found him and gave him soup and for a period of several weeks nursed him back to a reasonable state of health.

When he could walk well enough she gave him clothing and food and helped him to escape. He worked his way westward and while going along a road finally heard the sounds of battle. Then he spotted a German antitank gun and crew and went off the road and around them. Soon an American tank column appeared and he managed to stop the lead tank and warn them about the danger ahead. He climbed onto the tank in order to point out the place where the antitank gun was concealed, but a rifle bullet ricocheted off of the tank and hit him in the same place in his shoulder where he had been hit twice before. When finally his shoulder was operated on they pulled out pieces of shrapnel, skull, field jacket, and the rifle bullet.

Also he told me what had occurred on the morning of January 12 before we advanced against the enemy. He said that he had been on personal reconnaissance of the enemy positions before the rest of us arrived, and had learned that if we followed the existing plan we would be advancing exactly as the enemy would like us to. Along the far slope toward which we were to advance they had constructed three concrete and steel pillboxes about 200 hundred yards apart. Between them they had placed a row of tanks, dug in and painted white so they would blend into the snow. Observers in the pillboxes had an unrestricted view of the entire area in front of them, and were able to direct the fire of the tanks' cannons, and probably the fire of mortar emplacements, to bear on any point within the range of their binoculars. If we followed our plan of attack we would be advancing across open, snow-covered terrain which offered us no cover. In our dark uniforms, against the white snow, in broad daylight, we would be perfect targets for the enemy observers.

The Captain said that on returning from his reconnaissance he went immediately to the commanding officer of the battalion, the Lieutenant Colonel, and reported what he had learned. The Captain then requested permission to take our objective, which was the high ground west of the towns of Hatten and Rittershoffen, by going around the enemy's defenses; he stated that if we went as planned we would be decimated by artillery fire, and would have to withdraw without having even begun to reach our objective. The Lieutenant Colonel looked at his watch and replied that the Captain had his orders, and that he had 5 minutes to have his men begin the attack. Stunned, the Captain again made his case; the Lieutenant Colonel again looked at his watch, and replied that he now had three minutes to have his men begin the attack. The Captain made one final plea; the Lieutenant Colonel took one final look at his watch and replied that he now had only one minute to have his men begin the attack, and that afterwards he would be court-martialed for resisting orders.

The Captain told me he figured that if he refused to lead us he would be relieved of his command, and someone else would be made to do it who was unaware of the trap; so he decided he must. He said to me, "Well, I couldn't let you men go, and stay behind; I wouldn't have been able to live with myself." I do not remember if the Captain told me his reason for going against orders and having us halt and dig in when we reached the crest; perhaps he hoped that the Lieutenant Colonel would come out, see the situation, and change the plan, but this was not to be.

There are no words to express what my thoughts and feelings were as he talked; I was totally devastated. I can say now that, of course, when we men of the Battalion left the crest and walked down the slope we did not know what we were being sent into. We were prepared, as always, to meet and to fight the enemy, and knew as always that some of us might be wounded or killed. But we assumed, as always, that we would have a fighting chance... of winning... of surviving. We assumed, as we had to in order to keep our sanity, that even if our leaders could not allow themselves to think of us as persons, they would have to think of us as their means to victory, and, if only for that reason, would not knowingly waste us, would not knowingly trade our lives for nothing in return, as to do so would be to hurt their own program and to help that of the enemy.

The realization that our battalion commanding officer had sufficient information to know the consequences of the plan, and followed the plan anyway, was the greatest shock of my life. He could see that we would be advancing across open terrain which offered no cover. He could see that our dark uniforms against the white snow in broad daylight would be perfect targets. If he could not himself see the pillboxes and tanks, he should have believed that his combat-proven Captain had seen them. From our previous encounters with the enemy he was aware of the deadly accuracy and terrible destructiveness of their artillery, and that we could not possibly pass through their field of fire and reach our objective. And yet he refused to change the plan. It numbed me. To think of our walking trustfully down the slope... of the terrible scene when the explosions tore us into bloody pieces... of the indescribably horrible suffering which followed... and then to learn that it had all been avoidable was more than I could stand. I buried it deep down in the unknown recesses of my mind. Only many years later was I able to let myself remember and deal with it, and even then it was frightening, painful, and extremely difficult to do so.

But finally I could ask myself, "Why? Why did our commanding officer do it?" The quote from the Battalion History states that: "The Battalion was in the attack that was to have taken ground west of Hatten..." etc., indicating that our attack was part of a larger one. Apparently the Lieutenant Colonel had orders from his commanding officer that as part of a larger plan his battalion was to attack at a designated hour, and he was going by the clock. Since he told the Captain he would have him court-martialed for what he, the Lieutenant Colonel, thought of as resisting an order, perhaps he feared that if he asked permission to change the plan he would be court-martialed for resisting an order. Perhaps he felt that he had to be able to report that he had followed the plan. But in view of the new information he had received from his Captain's personal reconnaissance, that his own battalion was about to be destroyed by an enemy artillery barrage, why was he not able to have his battalion take a viable route to reach the objective? And why, as I later learned, was he promoted from Lieutenant Colonel to full Colonel?

Before I could let myself kill the man on the hillside I had to agree to it on the one condition: that if I got home I would work the rest of my life to end war and make sure that no one would ever be able to put me or anyone else in that position again. The knowledge of the position the entire battalion had been put in on January 12 made me not only reaffirm my vow, but make it stronger. How many other times during the war had "mistakes" like this occurred? To how many groups of brave men? Why did people let these persons acquire such power over them? Why did the people of nations listen to persons who told them they should pursue a policy of aggression against the people of other nations instead of cooperating with them? Why did they let such persons dictate their lives, and send them to their deaths? I had met so many wonderful, brave, loyal, sharing, loving, intelligent persons during the War. Why had we not been able to live our lives together in peace as we would have liked to? What are the real forces which determine the course of our destiny? Are we their helpless victims? These were the vital questions, and I was committed to finding the answers.

After 15 months of food, surgery, and physical therapy, I was able to get a pass from the hospital to go into town. The first shoe I received had been constructed in the hospital brace shop. Someone had taken a regular shoe and added to the sole and heel until it looked like the front end of a sperm whale. I was embarrassed to be seen in it, and when outside I would slink along on my crutches close to the walls of buildings. Then someone told me about Martin Larson, a man right there in Chicago who made a shoe that slanted down toward the toe so that it was much less noticeable. I bought a pair and was very relieved. In fact, in comparison to many, many other wounded I felt extremely lucky. Actually I felt lucky to be alive at all.

After 16 months I was discharged from the hospital, and from the Army, and returned to my home in Indianapolis. My physical wounds were not completely healed, but had reached a state where I could dress them myself. My left leg and right hand were working well enough, and the two and one half inches shortening of my leg was compensated by the built-up shoe.

The Aftermath

Although I was healing physically, during the time in the hospital and after returning to my home I was quite nervous. All I could think of was that we must never have another war, and that I must help to create a world where people would work with rather than against each other. Most people told me that the war was over, and that I should forget about it and go on with my life. They did not understand that I could not forget the war, and that working to create a peaceful world was the only way I could go on with my life.

So it was time to begin to keep my vow. But how? I realized that I did not know how, and that I must begin by obtaining information. My education had been interrupted by the war, so it seemed that I should pick up from where I left off and see where it would lead.

Before going into the Army I had been one year at Indiana University and thanks to the GI Bill I was able to return in the fall of 1946. During the first semester I learned three things: my nervousness made it very difficult for me to concentrate on the subject matter in my courses; IU was not the place to find the courses I needed; there was another university which was the place.

This discovery came as the result of reading an article in "LOOK" magazine. It began, "By the time you read this I will be in school in Bern, Switzerland on the GI Bill." GREAT! I really wanted to return to Europe. I had been jerked out of the war, and not having been able to be in on the finish I needed closure. Also, I felt uncomfortable in the States except when I could be with another combat veteran, and that did not happen very often. Research into the educational possibilities indicated that the place for me was the University of Geneva and its affiliate, the Graduate Institute of International Studies, in Switzerland. The material I sent for said that to enroll in the University I needed to have completed two years of college. Also, I needed to be able to understand and speak French.

During the second semester at IU I took French language courses and made the necessary arrangements with the Veterans Administration and the University of Geneva. Its rules were that if I passed the examinations after the first year at the University I could attend both it and the Graduate Institute for the next two years and, if I passed the final examinations, would receive an MA degree in Political Science and International Organization.

After finishing at IU in the summer of 1947 I boarded a ship and made my second crossing to France. It was a converted Liberty Ship, and though not like the famous ocean liners was incomparably more comfortable than the troopship had been, and there were no enemy submarines lurking below the surface. I did miss the thrill of seeing the huge convoy of great and small ships all around us, with the small destroyers racing in and out like greyhounds. As we came in to the northern French port of Cherbourg it was shocking to see the many sunken ships with their rusted topsides sticking out of the water. From there I went by rail to Geneva, and it was quite exciting to be actually traveling across France and seeing the sights along the way.

After getting settled in Geneva I took courses in the French language in the University's summer program for visitors, and began regular courses in the fall. They were in French, and I could understand him well though, but could not take notes. Fortunately the practice was for students to earn a little money by typing their notes and having the office of the *concierge* of the University sell them to the needy and give the money to the note-takers.

In the summer of 1948 I attended the French language course at the Sorbonne in Paris. The existentialist movement was in full swing and everyone from everywhere sat in sidewalk cafes under bright-colored umbrellas, and read newspapers, and argued, and drank everything, and smoked strong cigarettes, and wore berets and sandals, and the men wore beards.

On the first leg of my trip to Paris I took a train part way, and then rode my bike through my old battlefields. I found the large concrete pillbox I had been carried to, and it was an eerie feeling to be standing there alone in front of the steel door; with no soldiers, or guns, or tanks around, and no explosions. However, after I had returned to the road and was riding my bike again, there was a very loud explosion nearby. BOOM! Without thinking I crashed my bike into the ditch and covered my head with my hands. Then I realized that the war was over, and found that some French workers had set off explosives and blown up a pillbox a short distance away. It was twilight by then, and the road entered the Forest of Haguenau. As I rode along I kept half expecting to see a German tank come roaring and clanking out of the trees with cannon and machine guns blazing. No tank appeared, because World War II really was over.

My three years in Europe were wonderful in four ways: I learned much of what I needed to about how to stop war; made many wonderful friends both Swiss and from other countries including the States; there were so many wonderful places and art museums to visit; and I was able to downhill ski! I had always desired to, but after being injured had thought this would be impossible. However, after riding a bike up and down hills in Geneva for many months my leg seemed to be strong enough, and a Genevese bootmaker was kind enough to copy my left shoe and make a pair of ski boots. Just getting up into the incredibly beautiful Swiss and French Alps would have been wonderful enough, and learning to ski down them made it even more fantastic! I wasn't the greatest skier on the slopes, but I really enjoyed doing what I could.

All that was the good part, but I continued to be very nervous and usually very lonely. Actually I realize now that I was a mental and emotional basket case. I was full of wonderful love and hope on the one hand, and full of terrible anger and hate on the other. This Jekyll/Hyde conflict made my life a manic tragedy. I over or under reacted to everyone and everything. The crippling thing is that when one is emotionally disturbed and upset... from anger, fear, anxiety, or whatever... one cannot listen to others. Consequently one misunderstands, makes wrong assumptions, misinterprets what is occurring, and can not think or behave rationally. I should have been receiving therapy in a Veterans' Hospital; the outside wounds had been recognized, and treated, and had mostly healed, but the inside wounds were still raw. Of course I thought nothing was wrong with me that I could not handle myself. Big mistake.

I somehow managed to get through the required three years of courses at the University and the Graduate Institute, though it was amazing because I continued to find it very difficult to concentrate. In spite of all this I received my graduate degree in Political Science and International Studies in 1950 and headed for home on the beautiful ocean liner "Mauritania." Exciting experience. Back in the States I tried to work for peace. I went to Washington, D.C. and got on three Civil Service registers each of which qualified me for a position I was seeking in the State Department's Division of Exchange of Persons. While waiting for it I worked in the U.S. Department of Commerce, and after several months was told that they no longer had funding for the position. So I went to New York City and was hired by a non-profit agency working for peace.

In addition to the history and causes of war, such as political, economic, geographic, etc., the courses at the Graduate Institute had covered the structure and functions of the United Nations Organization (UN). At that time the great hope was that the UN would bring peace, cooperation, and prosperity to the people of Earth. For a while many persons put great energy into promoting ways to achieve these vital goals, but gradually hope and interest waned. Although the carefully worked out ideas which constituted the Charter of the UN were sane and workable, once WW II was over nationalism re-emerged with its ugly aims, fears, suspicions, and propaganda, and terrible new wars were begun, both "hot" and "cold." The former allies were now turning against each other, and it looked as if World War III might begin at any moment. Then in June of 1950 North Korea invaded South Korea and, as the saying goes, the rest is history.

Therefore the section of the UN on which we were depending to prevent war, the Security Council, could not even begin to fulfill its mission.

The failure of the Security Council after WW II and the onset of new wars made it an extremely depressing time for persons who were continuing to work for peace. I felt that I... that we... had reached a dead end. I was down and almost out. Then in the spring of 1957, in a corner drugstore (pharmacy) in Greenwich Village I noticed a fifty cent paperback book titled *Evolution In Action*. Out of curiosity I picked it up, began reading the Introduction, and could hardly believe my eyes. This was the knowledge I had been seeking! And finding it was the turning point in my life.

The author of the book was the late Sir Julian Huxley (1887-1973), world-famous biologist, writer, and teacher and the first person to become Director General of UNESCO, The United Nations Educational, Scientific, and Cultural Organization (an elective office). Put very briefly, what he wrote in his book is that:

> The Universe is a single, unified process of change (called *evolution*) occurring in three main phases: non-living; living; and human.

The first (non-living) phase began with an enormous explosion (the *Big Bang*), which created the area which we call "space." Within it were begun the three phases, one after another, with each phase having its own, unique method through which change occurs.

During the first (non-living) phase were formed the stars, galaxies, planets, etc., the method of change being mainly through a simple, very slow process of physical interaction.

The second (living) phase came out of the first phase with the emergence of the building blocks of life. The method of change in this phase is through biological mutation guided by natural selection, and its rate of change is much, much faster than that of the first phase.

The third (human) phase came out of the second phase with the emergence of our first human ancestors. Its method of change is through transmissible culture combined with conscious purpose, and its rate of change is again much, much faster. Thus the main unit of change and evolution in the human phase is not biological, but the stream of culture.

All three phases of the universal process of change (evolution) continue to occur today.

This entire concept of the Universe as being a Process of Change was new and very exciting to me, but two special features of the human phase of the Process were the most exciting of all, and, I felt, held the greatest promise for all persons on Earth.

One special feature is that the method of change is through "transmissible culture combined with conscious purpose." For the following reason, this feature is special: our culture consists of the ideas by which we live, and we ourselves create these ideas; therefore we can see that we have been, and are, creating and guiding the course of our own human destiny! During most of our human existence we could not be aware of these facts, but now that we can be aware of them we can purposely create ideas which will enable us to correct our present self-destructive course! That is, we can if we can acquire the information necessary to creating the appropriate ideas.

The other special feature of the human phase responds to this challenge, by showing that this phase is our actual Human Story, and that Huxley's model shows when, why, and how it began. This enables us to follow our Story from its beginning into the present time and see what actually occurred along the way, and that reveals what we desperately need to know today: how in the human beginning people created a successful culture and put themselves on a successful course; how they then inadvertently changed their culture into an unsuccessful one, and put themselves on the self-destructive course on which we, their descendants, find ourselves today (which includes our self-destructive habit of making war on each other).

The possible happy result of our having acquired all of this information is that we can use it to create ideas by which we can correct our present desperate situation.

My first problem became that, although I had located the point where our story began, I could not follow it from then because I did not have the necessary information. After much research I obtained it and began to write an outline of our Human Story. On completing it I found that it does show how humans put themselves on a successful course, lost it, and can now regain it, and that this information does include the causes of war and how they can now be eliminated.

Epilogue

In the summer of 1981 my wife Mary Lue and I and our two daughters Karen and Jill, aged 20 and 17, went to Europe for a vacation. For nine weeks we backpacked in France, Switzerland, Italy, Austria, Germany, and England, and had a wonderful time.

One evening in Geneva we were sitting around a table in an outdoor café making plans for the next day. A man and a woman were the only other persons there, and after a while the man approached us saying that he would like to meet some fellow Americans. He seemed amiable so we invited him and the woman to join us. They were very pleasant and soon we were involved in an interesting conversation. We learned that he, Phil, was an American who had served in Europe in WW II, and she, Rena, was a German who had lived in Germany all through the war. She was his wife and spoke English so I told them that I too had served in Europe. At that point their teenage son arrived but could not stay because he had to go to their hotel room to feed his dog. As the young man was tall, handsome, charming and spoke English our daughters escaped with him.

The four of us drank beer and talked and talked until the café closed, and then went to a bar and drank beer and talked and talked until the bar closed. We told war stories and bonded. One of the things Phil told us was that he had been a crew member of a B-17 Bomber and that after several missions on the same plane he had been called for other duty and missed the next mission. During it the plane was hit by enemy fire and exploded in flames killing all on board. He joined another crew and flew more missions, but even so he suffered from a feeling that he should have been with his buddies. In an effort to recover from this feeling, when the war was over he searched military cemeteries until he had found the graves of each one of his crew, who had been identified by their dog tags. He decided to live in Germany and took a position with "The Stars and Stripes" military newspaper in the city of Darmstadt, and there he met and married Rena.

They learned that from Geneva we were going to Italy, Austria, Germany, and England before returning to the States, so they said that during our travels we must stay at their home in Darmstadt, and we accepted their invitation. Then we went to their hotel room and got our daughters and the two families said, "Auf Wiedersehen." Florence, Venice, and Salzburg were wonderful, and so were the old towns along the "Romantic Road" in Germany. Then we arrived in Darmstadt and went to the home of our new friends. Next day was beautiful so they invited us to go for a drive. As their VW flatback held only five persons Rena drove the four of us to Heppenheim where I had been a POW, and I got out and walked alone through the front door of the reception building into which I had been carried on a stretcher. Bearers had put down my stretcher on the floor just inside, and when I stood on the spot where I had lain in lonely misery I knew it had all really happened. Eerie.

Then Rena drove us to her old home town nearby and showed us the graves of her young school friends who had been killed during a bombing raid. When the sirens sounded they had gone down into their cellars with their families for safety, but fire bombs burned the oxygen out of the air and they were all suffocated. Instead of going into their cellar Rena's father took his family up into the hills and they all survived.

The graves of Rena's school friends were in one section, and looking at the grouping of the headstones I imagined a school room of students sitting at their desks next to each other, full of life and hope. Hearing the story and seeing the graves of these innocent victims of war made us feel very sad.

In the same cemetery side by side in a row were six graves of German soldiers, and seeing their headstones standing next to each other in a line made me think of them as comrades fighting and dying together for a cause they had been misled to believe in. As a soldier who had killed other soldiers, seeing these small monuments which had been carefully placed there by those who loved these dead men gave me a very sad and strange feeling.

However, sharing these deep emotional experiences made the five of us survivors feel very close to each other.

Next day brought more beautiful, sunny weather so Phil drove us north and across the Rhine River and then down the valley of the Mosel River. Famous for its white wine, the valley's high, steep hills on both sides are covered by vineyards, and as we drove along we passed through one picturesque town after another. We stopped at one where a wine festival was in progress, tasted the delicious wine, and being moved by the fun and excitement around us joined a colorful procession.

Then Phil drove us across a bridge to another town and turned up a winding driveway to a two story stone house and parked the car. He led us to the front of the house and up some stone steps onto an open porch where a man and two older and two younger women were sitting. They looked up at us in surprise and we were embarrassed because we felt that we were intruding on their Sunday afternoon quiet time. Of course they and Phil were good friends and he immediately approached the man and they shook hands and exchanged a few words in German. Then the man spoke in German to the four women and they all rose and the younger of the two older women, who was the wife and mother, welcomed us in English and we all sat down. Phil asked me what battle I had been in when I was wounded, and when I told him the man's eyes widened and he said in German, "So was I!" We had actually fought against each other. Phil was equally surprised because he had not known this.

Suddenly everything changed. First they had to see where I had been hit in the leg. Then they all went into the house and came back with trays of food and drink. The grandmother did not speak English but the mother, Helga, did and we began to have an exciting conversation. Then the man, Wilfried, took me by the arm and led me upstairs and showed me his war souvenirs. He understood English a bit and spoke a few words, and I knew a bit of German. He was two months younger than me and during the war had been in training as a glider pilot and then was put in the infantry. Toward the end of the war he was captured by American soldiers and picked up some English from them as a POW.

On the top of a high hill overlooking the town there was a picturesque ruin of an old castle which had been preserved and the ground floor made into a vintage restaurant. Our hosts insisted that we all go there for supper as their guests, so we all went and had a wonderful time together in spite of the language difficulties. Afterward they asked when we would be leaving Darmstadt and arranged with Phil for us to take a bus to their town and have Wilfried drive us down the Mosel Valley to Trier where we would board a train for England.

Our Darmstadt hosts showed us some more sights in and around their city, and after a week we said auf Wiedersehen, hugged goodbye, took the bus to meet Wilfried, and drove with him to Trier. Helga was already there so we all had lunch, visited Roman ruins, and then had another emotional parting. We exchanged Christmas cards every year with both families.

It seems that our family's European adventure can be considered to be a plus factor toward seeing The Human Experiment as being successful.

PART II
Our New
Human Story

Introduction
The Four Paradises

Accounts have been passed down through time saying that long ago there was a place on Earth which was a human paradise. Whether it really existed or was merely a tale was long talked about, but no one had evidence which could prove it one way or the other. Finally the evidence in our actual Human Story offers the proof, and what it reveals is amazing. Not only did the paradise exist, but it was the second one in a series of three, and we are in the process of creating a fourth!

Of course it can seem unrealistic (putting it mildly) to say that we are in the process of creating a human paradise on Earth, when we have been over-populating our planet and destroying its life-sustaining natural environment as fast as we could, killing each other in terrible wars that have not even been declared, letting deadly diseases become pandemic, following "leaders" who divided us instead of bringing us together and have been taking us down the road to self-destruction, and so on. It is understandable that this horrible, irrational, morbid situation is causing many persons to despair, thinking that we have proved ourselves to be merely another "unsuccessful species" and that it is too late to save ourselves from going the way of the dinosaurs.

Fortunately, however, we can now see that there is another side to our human reality, which is that we are a *successful* species, but that we could not recognize this until we had discovered our actual Human Story. It shows us something we desperately need to know today, which is that our first human ancestors knowingly took certain mental, vocal, and physical steps and thereby unknowingly began an *experiment in living* which was new on planet Earth and possibly new in the entire Universe.

As noted, this radically new "Human Experiment" by our ancestors was to see if by using their new type of brain structure they could create cooperative ideas in their minds which they could communicate to each other through developing their potential for vocal language. If so, together they could cooperate consciously to improve their ability to survive and to enjoy life. What everyone on planet Earth needs to recognize now is that this experiment begun by our early ancestors was completely *successful.*

However, we need to see also that our later human ancestors were unable to continue the experiment successfully because they could not recognize the *reasons* for the initial human success. Our actual Human Story reveals these reasons, and enables us to see what we can do now in order to again make our Human Experiment a successful one.

Very fortunately we have developed a global communication system which makes possible the instantaneous, worldwide dissemination of our new information, so that everyone can have access to it. That will enable each person to see why we could not have recognized and entered the *fourth paradise* until now. Our Story presents all of this vital information in a clear, understandable way, and enables us to fulfill what shall be seen as constituting our wonderful, natural, human destiny.

To begin our Story, let us proceed to the building of the First Human Paradise.

Chapter I
The First Paradise

Let us imagine that we have traveled far back in time to a beautiful spring morning in southeast Africa. We are members of a group of eleven persons who have left the safety of a clump of trees and are out on the grassy plain gathering food. The bright sunshine reflects off the tall grass as it moves in the warm breeze, making the grassy plain, the *savannah*, resemble the rolling waves of an ocean. Large birds circle silently high overhead and small birds flit from one place to another chirping their songs.

While breathing in the clean air of nature we watch the persons around us sweep the plain with their eyes, then look down into the grass, then look out on the plain again, in a continuing cycle. Following their example we see a small herd of some kind of animal moving in the distance. Near us we notice a small boy who is learning how to imitate his mother. He watches her squat down and lift a nest in which are two brown eggs. She holds the nest in her lap, opens an egg, and pours the liquid into her mouth. Next she opens the other egg and pours the liquid into the boy's mouth. Then the two move with the rest of us farther out onto the plain, where we find and eat whatever edible things lie in our path, the boy taking two steps for every one by his mother.

Suddenly someone gives the scream which means: *Danger! Run to the trees!* The mother grabs her child, and holding him under one arm runs as fast as she can toward the clump of trees. We run alongside her, and when there is another scream no one looks back to see the throat of a loved one being mangled in the bloody jaws of a leopard; this has been witnessed too many times before. We keep running until we reach a tree with a branch near the ground. We help the mother and child up onto it, and she carries him quickly up as far into the branches as she can and we follow her up. Other group members climb up into other trees. Trembling and sad, we watch the victim's body being dragged away, but we know that we were unable to do anything to prevent the death. We wait awhile, then descend to the ground and resume our interrupted search for food.

On returning through time to ourselves in the present it is easy to see that these early ancestors of ours would have been unhappy about their inability to defend themselves: they lacked the jaws, claws, weight, strength, speed, fangs, coils, wings, beaks, and talons of their adversaries, and could not climb, dig, nor bite well. Fortunately, both for them and for us their descendants, they developed their own way to defend themselves. To see how these early persons achieved this let us follow their inspiring story.

Our knowledge of them comes from our discoveries of bones, skulls, foot and hand prints, rock and cave painting, and primitive tools and weapons, plus the findings of molecular biology. With this information, plus studies of primitive groups living in recent times, studies of animals in nature, and knowledge of ourselves, we can reconstruct much about these early persons and their lives.

They lived in the natural environment surrounded by deadly dangers and were held together by their common fear of them. Instinctively and consciously they knew they desperately needed each other's help in order to survive, and therefore treated each other with respect. Because they depended on the natural environment to produce their food they had to move around to find it, so were forced to live together in small, mobile groups. When a group became too large some of the persons would form another group and move to another area.

They had developed the ability to use bones, sharp stones, and pieces of tree branches as tools (such as for digging edible roots) and weapons (such as for killing small animals). Also they had begun to communicate with each other through sign language and basic vocal language, i.e. to "talk" to each other. All of these were vital steps because they led to their becoming able to make and carry out cooperative group plans (ideas) for defensive and offensive actions which greatly improved their ability to obtain food, survive, and enjoy life.

As time passed they kept improving their proficiency to communicate through vocal and sign language and to create new ideas for cooperative group plans. Through these advances, plus improving their skill in making and using tools and weapons, including clubs and sharp spears and stones, they became able to hunt and kill small and some medium-sized animals for food and hides.

To see what this led to, let us imagine that we are members of a group of fifteen such persons on a summer evening. As the sunlight fades we climb into trees with branches suitable to be sleeping places, relatively safe from night-time predators. In the morning we descend to the ground, leave the safety of the trees, and venture onto the vast open grassland to search for food. After walking for awhile in the bright sunlight we have collected some eggs, berries, and nuts when we see a small antelope lying in the grass. Although wounded it manages to struggle up and limp away from us until its path takes it into a rock formation where it becomes trapped. We follow and kill it with our clubs and spears, and are cutting it into pieces with our sharp knives of stone when suddenly we realize that our situation has been reversed! A leopard has entered the rock formation and blocks our escape; we have changed from being the trappers to being the trapped!

As the beast slowly approaches us, snarling through bared fangs, shifting yellow eyes from one to the other of us, we are terrified. All that each of us can think of is to run from this killer, because that is what our people have done instinctively for many thousands of years, but we can not climb the sheer rock walls on three sides of us. Had we not been so frightened we might have thought to hurl the meat to the leopard, but what each of us does think is, "I'm going to be killed!" and stark terror holds us frozen in place. Then suddenly someone screams and throws a sharp stone which hits the leopard in the side. As this has never happened to it before, surprise causes it to stop momentarily in its tracks and turn its head to see what hit it. Immediately we all join the attack, screaming and hurling our bone and wooden clubs and sharp spears and stones at our enemy and then picking up and throwing rocks at it, one hitting it in an eye. This unprecedented act of group aggression causes the leopard to reconsider and quickly withdraw.

We are astounded! We can not believe what we have done. For a moment we fall silent and can only stare at the place where the leopard had been. Then we begin to yell and jump up and down and hug each other. Using vocal, sign, and body language, during the days that follow we re-enact our great victory, again and again, pretending that a large stone is the leopard.

The question we ask each other is, "Could we do it again; not because of being trapped, but deliberately?" The question we ask ourselves is, "Could *I* do it again? It was one thing for me to fight when there was no escape. But if I could run and escape, along with most of the others, it is quite another thing for me to imagine myself standing against the terrible fangs and slashing claws of an enemy whom I mortally fear and have always run from. But what if we all run next time and I am the one who gets caught and killed?"

Each of us is very proud of what he or she has done, and has a strong desire to be able to do it again. In response to our compelling need to defeat the leopard, and our strong belief that we can succeed, we plan our defense and each of us makes a daring promise to the others: "The next time we are attacked, I will stand and fight."

We begin immediately to prepare ourselves for a future attack so that when the moment comes we will be ready. We know that none of us could stand alone against the leopard, but we believe that if instead of running we stay together and all shout and use our weapons we can drive off or perhaps kill our attacker. Because each of us helped to drive off the leopard before, we believe that we can trust ourselves and each other to keep the promise to do it again.

A few days later a leopard picks up our scent and follows it toward the place where we are resting in the grass. When our lookout sees it he runs to us saying that the moment has come. Our greatest desire as individuals is to be able to hold in our minds the shared idea that our best way to survive is to stand together with our companions and fight, rather than succumb to instinctive fear and flee in terror. As the leopard approaches it slows its pace, confused by our not running and consequently not allowing it to select a victim to chase; but it keeps coming right up to us, baring its fangs and snarling. Suddenly, according to plan, we all begin to yell and scream, and while some of us use both hands to hold out our long, sharp spears and keep the beast away, others throw their clubs and sharp stones. It snarls, and tries to bat the spears away, and takes one in its jaws, but two other spears immediately jab it, and then two more. Adrenalin rush, strong desire to overcome the enemy, sense of pride and loyalty, and maximum use of outer skill and inner strength enable each of us to succeed. We hold the idea in our minds, act on it, and together drive off the very surprised, bleeding leopard. We have won!

Flushed with victory, and ecstatically happy, we sing and dance for joy. We each know that we have changed our lives forever. No longer will the leopard decide who will live and who will die; we have taken that power away from it. By creating an idea which enabled us to change our thinking and behavior, we forced it to change its thinking and behavior. Now none of us will die, or at least each will have a fighting chance.

Alone, no one of us could have accomplished this, but by each of us participating in making and carrying out the group plan we could succeed.

Returning to the present we can see that this new ability of our ancestors to defend themselves from a fearful enemy made a revolutionary difference in their lives. In that moment they delivered themselves from being helpless prey and took the first step toward becoming the mightiest hunters on Earth. No longer the helpless, frightened victims of powerful enemies, they could deal with them on an equal basis. Each of them had made a quantum jump in his or her personal ability to survive and enjoy being alive, and thereby in self-confidence and self-esteem. For each of them it was... *paradise.*

Today we would not desire to live as they did without the safety factors and material comforts available to us, and our story goes on to show that in the second paradise this began to be remedied. However, the persons who created the first paradise were accustomed to living as they did materially, and to them what they added to their way of life was what they most desired: the ability to protect themselves in their daily lives, especially while gathering and hunting food.

It can seem that as individual persons they might have felt that they had given up their freedom to do whatever they desired to do whenever they chose to, but for the following reasons that probably was not the case. Long before attaining the first paradise they cared instinctively about each other's safety and well-being, were instinctively cooperative, and within their group had developed a natural level of friendship, loyalty, and trust. In this social structure, surrounded by the dangers of the natural environment, a baby, child, and adolescent developed to become an adult person who valued being a member of such a supportive group. In a word, what they had been experiencing and enjoying from the human beginning was what today we call *community*.

Then by developing their potential for vocal language they became able to make plans through use of which they raised instinctive cooperation, friendship, loyalty, trust, and community to the level of consciousness. This thrilled them because it made each person in the group feel even more needed and essential, more in control of his or her life, and more free. For example, they had not desired to let someone in their group be killed by the leopard, and they had chosen to free themselves from having to let that happen.

To understand "instinctive cooperation," we need to see that our genes have their own agenda, which is to get themselves into the next generation, and the next, and so on, i.e. to be immortal. Therefore it has been said that we are merely "taxicabs for our genes." However, because we pass our genes on through sexual intercourse, and this a cooperative act, natural selection has caused in us a genetic infrastructure which not only motivates us to have the urge to have sexual intercourse, and has made it a highly enjoyable experience, but which enables us to develop the friendship, loyalty, and trust which makes other cooperation possible. Thus, though our genes are entirely "selfish," it has been in their interest as well as ours for us to become increasingly cooperative.

The persons in the human line had unknowingly been moving toward the creation of the first paradise ever since they descended from the trees to the ground, stood up, and ran and walked on two legs. That freed their arms, hands, fingers and thumbs from being used for locomotion and instead being used for many other actions which, without their knowing it, helped to develop their brains and minds to think in new creative ways. Then through developing vocal language they raised instinctive cooperation to the level of conscious cooperation and created the first human paradise.

It was a *personal* paradise, because it was the result of a plan conceived and carried out by the individual person to help him or her self. Obviously one could not have conceived nor carried out the plan in isolation; one had to accomplish this in conjunction with the other persons in the group. Nevertheless it was an individual act. *Each* person had to form the group plan (idea) in his or her own mind and make the decision to act on it, and then do so on his or her own: no one could do it for someone else. What they were learning was that cooperation is actually a matter of what we call today "enlightened self-interest." Of course they were thinking too of the welfare of their loved ones, and that increased their incentive to participate in the plan because it included each person in the group and made each person an essential, valued member, treated with respect by the others.

All this was in fact necessary because it was learned from experience that the group plans could be successful only if each person participated in creating them and in carrying them out. For that to happen each person had to be highly motivated not only to cooperate but to do so voluntarily, in spite of the great personal risks both physical and mental, the latter because each had to be able to trust the intelligence, loyalty, and courage of the others. The creation of this conscious type of cooperative government, this "paradise," was a monumental step never before taken on planet Earth (as far as we know), nor possibly in the entire Universe.

In driving off the leopard our ancestors took the first decisive step toward advancing what we have called the "Human Experiment," which was to see if they could use their new brain structure to create new survival ideas, and put them into practice, on a continuing basis. As we shall see, they were able to achieve this, and in doing so they attained the basic *goal* of each human person, which was to continually improve their ability to survive and enjoy life. The *method* through which individual persons brought the idea of this into their consciousness was by participating with the others in the group in developing and using vocal language. The conscious goal and method were uniquely human, and as we follow our Human Story we shall see that by having the goal and using the method humans have three times built a human paradise, the second and third times on the foundation of its predecessor.

Because each paradise was lost, without being fully conscious of it humans have been striving to build a fourth paradise. We have made real progress, but even with all of our great accomplishments, we will see that we could not have succeeded until now, the main reason being that we had not yet acquired the necessary *information*. Consequently we could not know what we needed to about our past, nor about our brain structure and Culture, and could not recognize the possibility of a fourth paradise, and could not be aware that we are now in a position to live in it. To see why we are, we need first to look at the background to Chapter 1.

Chapter 2
Background

The background information is in two brief interrelated sections. First, the general steps from pre-human to human, and second the specific steps in the origin and development of our brain.

Section 1: Seven to five million years ago in eastern Africa a single biological mutation occurred in our first human ancestor. Most mutations do not survive, but this one did, or we would not be here today... something resembling us perhaps, but not us.

The bones we have found show that this first successful human beginning occurred in a type of animal we call an *ape*. Its mutation was passed on and began the branch of our family tree which we call *hominids*, which means bi-pedal (upright walking) apes. Other mutations kept occurring in this line, and the ones that gave survival advantage were preserved, and about 1.8 million years ago a group of advanced hominids called *Homo erectus* appeared. They had so many human qualities that today they can be considered to have been the first humans, and they may have been the people referred to in the previous chapter as having defeated the leopard.

Their landscape (the Great Rift Valley of east Africa) was a tropical mixture of small woodlands, and vast grasslands called *savannas*, with occasional mountain ranges.

These people were taller than their predecessors, as tall as 5' 6", and bigger brained, 900 to 1100 cubic centimeters, but smaller than our average modern brain, 1350 c.c. Still, they were able to fashion wooden spears and to chip stone into beautiful hand axes. At some point they may have hunted large animals, which requires efficient weapons and elaborate social cooperation, although they probably had only the most rudimentary speech. Perhaps 20 percent of their calories came from meat. They established home bases, and cared for dependent infants.

They probably made the critical transition from the male and female hierarchies of chimp society to the spousal bonds of modern men and women. Erect people also learned to overcome their instinctive fear of fire and to control its use.

Probably seeking food, some groups of the erect people began to move northward and out of Africa, taking their fire with them. This occurred about 1.2 million to 700,000 years ago, during a warm, wet period when the Sahara Desert had enough rainfall for groups to cross it safely. Eventually their descendants moved into Europe, the Near East, parts of northern Asia, and tropical southern and southeastern Asia. They could not inhabit extremely cold places (i.e. most of northern Eurasia), and they did not reach Australia or the Americas. During their time the sabre-toothed tiger became extinct.

These early Homo erectus persons can be grouped by three different places: Homo erectus in Europe, including the Mediterranean region; Homo erectus in eastern Asia; and Homo erectus remaining in eastern Africa and mutating to become Homo sapiens (i.e. us).

1. The *Homo erectus* persons in Europe who went north and mutated to become *Neanderthals* are in the fossil record from about 130,000 to 28,000 years ago, thus originating before the start of the last ice age about 90,000 years ago. They were the first persons to adapt successfully to life on the edge of an ice age world. More bones of Neanderthals have been found than of any other hominid group, including some thirty nearly complete skeletons. They are named for the Neander Valley skeleton found near Dusseldorf, Germany in 1856. They had a bulky, squat physique with heavy muscles and barrel chests in men, women, and children, to offset the cold. Males were about 5 feet six inches tall and weighed about 155 pounds, while females were about five feet two inches and about 120 pounds. Their brains were at least as large as our own, although shaped differently. Their skulls were long and low, like those of earlier people, with a notable ridge above the eyes and a massive nasal opening, larger than other persons before or since.

As tool makers, Neanderthals did not change their designs over tens of thousands of years. From stone they made borers, scrapers, points, knives, and hand axes. They could hunt wooly mammoths, musk oxen, wolves, cave bears, wild horses, and reindeer, and lived mainly on a diet of hunted animal meat. They used fire, scraped hides for clothing and shelter, and buried their dead, the first people known to have done so. Bodies are found in association with tools, but there is no pattern of other burial goods nor any clue of ceremonies. Some skeletons show marks of illness or injury that occurred sometime before death, so there must have been social care for disabled individuals. The position of their larynx suggests that they could not make as many sounds as modern humans, but the extent of vocal language is not known. Studies are being made of their DNA taken from bones from 30,000 years ago. There is disagreement among experts as to whether these indicate that Neanderthals may or may not have been ancestral to us. In any case, it is clear that they were a specialized form of Homo erectus adapted to extreme cold.

2. The *Homo erectus* people who went to eastern Asia were the first hominids to arrive, and there they developed distinctive adaptions to the forest environments of tropical and temperate Asia. Forests rather than grasslands meant that people had to keep moving in order to find fruits and nuts. Instead of stone for their tools, they used bamboo and wood, raw materials that are not preserved in ancient sites. These Homo erectus forest cultures flourished and evolved slowly over hundreds of thousands of years, quite independently, it seems, of changes in humankind in Africa and Europe. Homo erectus persons seem to have lasted several thousand years longer in Asia than in Europe and Africa, but eventually were replaced by Homo sapiens.

3. The *Homo erectus* people who remained in eastern Africa, and over time mutated to become us, i.e. *Home sapiens*. (Homo = bipedal primates + sapiens = wise).

Using their superior brains and language abilities they gradually replaced the remaining groups of hominids in Africa and reached a population of perhaps 50,000 by around 100,000 years ago.

Section 2: To understand our Story from this point on, we need to begin to consider the origin, evolution, and development of the brain.

To begin we can recall J. Huxley's model of the Universe as being a process of change occurring in three main phases: non-living (or inorganic); living (or organic); and human (or psychosocial). The first phase began with the "Big Bang," as a result of which Space was formed, and in it the galaxies of stars, planets, etc. began to form; the second phase came out of the first phase with the emergence of the building blocks of life; the third phase came out of the second phase with the emergence of human beings; and all three phases continue to occur today.

We can begin to consider the origin of the brain as occurring during the second (living) phase of the Universe with the emergence of small sea-animals, such as jellyfish, which had a pre-brain composed of a group of neurons called "ganglia." Then there emerged fishes with spines (backbones) and the neurons gradually were guided through the spine to the head and began to form a true brain which acted as a central nervous system. It evolved and developed in a series of land-living animals and eventually became the human brain.

Next we can turn to the work of the eminent neuro-scientist Dr. Paul MacLean (1913-2007), who for six decades was Chief of the Department of Brain Evolution and Behavior at the U.S. National Institutes of Health (NIH), one of the great research centers of our time. The background is that during his research MacLean recognized three brains (neural systems) in our head and noticed striking similarity between them and the brains in the heads of the three major animal groups of evolution: reptilian, old mammalian, and new mammalian. For more than half a century he and his team traced these parallels and showed how each of our three human brains matches a brain developed during each of these evolutionary epochs.

The picture which emerges is that in Nature a system that works is never abandoned; instead new, enlarged, and more efficient systems are built upon the old, forming a composite system. In brain evolution, on top of an early land-adapting animal's brain a "cortex"(from the Latin word for bark) began to form and eventually covered it and became a new, "reptilian" brain. Over it a cortex formed and became the old mammalian brain, and over it a cortex formed and became the new mammalian brain (or neocortex). The role of each new brain was to correct problems in an older brain and/or to expand its possibilities.

MacLean called the combination of reptilian, old mammalian, and new mammalian brains the "triune brain," and found that it operates like three interconnected, cooperating, biological computers, each with its own special intelligence, its own subjectivity, its own sense of time and space, and its own memory. Following are very brief descriptions of the three brains (which today form the basis of our composite human brain):

The Reptilian Brain, called by MacLean the "R-complex," is the oldest and most primitive "mentally" of the three, and yet was an enormous advance over previous brains. It includes the brain stem and cerebellum, and its basic function is to keep the body alive and well. This "first" brain controls muscles, balance, and autonomic functions, such as breathing, heartbeat, digestion, and the execution of the "fight or flight" response to stress (danger). It functions in a habitual, patterned way and is unable to alter either inherited or learned behavior.

It can, however, take over the physical parts of a learned skill such as typing, ice skating, bike riding, driving a car, or the sensory-motor aspects of playing a piano, thereby freeing our higher brains to stand outside of the immediate motor action as observers, which can permit them to discover ways to improve.

The *Old Mammalian Brain* covers the Reptilian Brain and this "second" brain is concerned with emotions and cognition, and is infinitely more complex and discriminating. Everything is either agreeable or disagreeable; survival depends on avoidance of pain and repetition of pleasure.

The *New Mammalian Brain (Neocortex/Verbal-Intellectual)* covers the two earlier brains, and is divided into left and right hemispheres joined together by the corpus callosum, a thick band of nerve fibers. The left half controls the right side of the body and the right half controls the left side of the body; the right brain is more spatial, abstract, musical, and artistic, while the left brain is more linear, rational and verbal.

This high, "third" brain introduced language and thinking, the ability to stand outside all other activities of the brain and observe these activities objectively and consider all factors of a situation rather than react to them from instinct alone. It occupies five times more skull space than the reptilian brain and the old mammalian brain combined, covers them, and consists of some hundred billion neurons, each of which is capable of interacting with upward of a hundred thousand other neurons to form fields of coordinated neural action. There are no limits to what our third brain can translate, from input from the world outside to imagination and thought within. With the development of this third brain there was opened an infinitely wide window of awareness.

The first brain registers present tense only. The second brain computes both present and past. With the addition of the third brain, came awareness of the past, present, and future, and this new dimension broadened our awareness greatly. However, its tendency toward continual expansion of awareness and experience can help or hurt us. This intellectual-creative brain introduces language and creative imagination, which is the foundation of all organized thought and creative intelligence, but it can also cause us to imagine things which are not accurate and, if believed, can put one on a wrong course.

Because each new brain can think of more and better ways to survive, it is "smarter" than its predecessor, and has gained a degree of control over it, but must accommodate its still vitally important workings. For instance, our old mammalian brain is "smarter" than our reptilian brain but must support it in its original job of maintaining the systems which keep us alive, including breathing, digestion, circulation, etc.

The striking differences among these three brains can also help us or hurt us. When the three are integrated and functioning together cooperatively, and therefore in harmony, they give us the ability to think clearly and solve our human problems. When integration fails, our mind becomes "a house divided against itself" and can make decisions which can be very detrimental to our well-being.

MacLean next described a *fourth* brain in our head, the *prefrontal cortex* (prefrontal lobes), located immediately behind the ridge of our brow. While our reptilian brain has modules or parts that are hundreds of millions of years old, indications are that our prefrontal cortex began to develop effectively only some 40,000 years ago. MacLean attributed to it our "higher human virtues of love, compassion, empathy, and understanding, as well as our advanced intellectual skills."

Chapter 3
Ideas and the first
Wrong Change in Course

Our early human ancestors began to use their new survival tools well in their natural homeland of east Africa. They used their new three-part brain to study what was occurring in the natural environment around them, and inside their group, and formed and shared ideas about these occurrences.

For example, experience taught them that for their group plan to be successful it was necessary for each of them to participate in forming it, and that was the origin of the idea of what we call *democracy*. Another vital element was each person's promise to do his or her part in carrying out a plan because this was necessary to its success, and that was the beginning of the idea of the *human social contract*, which included ideas such as courage, commitment, duty, honor, and justice.

Rather than competing with each other to create a hierarchy of *individuals* inside their group, as animals do instinctively in order to dominate each other, people used their new brains, minds, vocal language, and reason, to create a hierarchy of *ideas* inside their group, so as to minimize the instinctive rivalry for supremacy, and maximize the instinctive proclivity to work together, in order to become able to dominate the animals who lived *outside* their group.

In addition to using reason to create cooperative plans (ideas) to overcome the leopard, they used it to create other ideas and plans for cooperative actions, and passed them from one generation to the next, continually adding to and improving them and adding them to the body of shared ideas which we call the human "Culture." Because each person in the group participated in creating and improving the plans and other ideas, together they were creating a Culture which was benevolent, one which included, accepted, and helped each person, a joyous Culture. Thus, forming and using the human Culture as their vehicle to carry forward and improve their vital plans and ideas was another plus factor toward success for The Human Experiment.

It is crucial for us to recognize that, because each person knew that he or she desperately needed the help of the other persons in the group in order to survive, each person desired that the other persons develop to be as capable as possible, and helped them in this. A modern-day example of this practice is that each of the members of an athletic team desires to become as accomplished a player as he/she can, and desires also that the others become as accomplished players as possible and helps them in this so that the team can win. (If one can not learn to become a "team-player," one is dismissed from the team.)

The Culture was created in and existed only in the mind of each participating person, but at that time no one could recognize its existence. Nevertheless, the Culture was brought into being in their individual minds, and in this sense was a part of each person. At the same time, because it was the product of all their minds, it had an existence separate from each person and in this sense had a life of its own... although at that time no one could recognize that either. As humans created their culture, it created them, in an ongoing, feedback relationship, and in this way they guided and became personally responsible for the course of their personal lives and their human destiny... although at that time no one could recognize that either.

Their first concern had to be in what was occurring nearest to them, in order to be aware of present danger. At the same time, because they lived in the open they were highly aware of what was occurring above them: the rising and setting of the sun and the moon, thunder, wind, rain, and flashes of lightning that sometimes hit the ground and caused the occasional grass fires. Studies of modern "primitives" indicate that the early persons thought of these natural elements as being forces much greater than themselves, were in awe of them, gave them names, and talked to each other about them in an effort to understand them.

We can not know exactly how their minds worked nor what they thought, but we can see that there are various possibilities, the most basic one being simply that they would respond in some way. Examples might be: it is cold during the night, but the sun warms me in the morning; the sun makes me hot in the afternoon, so I need some shade; the lightning is scary and dangerous, so I need to hide from it.

By naming all of the natural forces, and making up and telling stories about them, persons were trying to understand why each force acted as it did, in order to feel a degree of control over it, such as becoming able to predict its actions. Although their vocal language was rudimentary, added to it was the storyteller's ability to evoke excitement through facial expressions and use of arms and hands and sometimes of the whole body, perhaps doing dance steps and/or singing, and probably the group would join in. Probably rhythms were made through hand clapping, and eventually hitting a stick against another stick or a hollow log, and much later making a drum and hitting it with a stick or their hands.

Lacking the information about the workings of Nature which it has taken their descendants many thousands of years to accumulate, it seems that the only way they could approach storytelling would be to assume that a natural force was like them, but much greater and more powerful, and yet did things for the same reasons that they would. After sleeping all night the sun rose early in the morning, and after a long day was tired and again went to sleep. Then the night sneaked in like a leopard, and they named and probably feared it. The moon liked to visit different places, and sometimes would come up where they could see it, and sometimes not. Thus they began the human, "anthropomorphic" practice of ascribing human form or attributes to non-human entities. ("Anthropo" comes from Greek *anthropos,* meaning "human being," and "morphic" comes from Greek. *morphic,* meaning "form.").

As the sun was the most consistently prominent force perhaps they thought it had the most power. Perhaps they imagined that sometimes it became angry and made the sky dark and unleashed the wind, rain, lightning, and thunder.

Next might have been: The sun makes me too hot, I wish today were cooler. Then: I wish I could make it cooler. Then: I will ask the sun to make the day cooler. Eventually a dance to appeal to the sun was created, and also ones to appeal to the moon, night, clouds, rain, or whatever: the beginning of *religion.* (The word comes from the Latin *religare,* "to bind," here meaning the bond between humans and the natural forces.)

They may or may not have formed a general concept of a single force greater than themselves which caused everything, and, if they did, they may or may not have named it. But it seems sure that they would have named each natural force and made up stories to explain its existence and actions.

Of course there were many other reasons for their telling stories. One was simply that they liked entertainment. Another probably was that the storyteller liked being the center of attention for a while and gaining in status as an important member of the group. Another reason was for adults to teach children what they wanted them to know, such as how to not become separated from the group, how to cooperate with its other members, how to make and use tools and weapons, etc. But there was a deeper reason for all this mental activity, which was that while developing the *ability* to reason and understand, they were developing a *need* to reason and understand, which continues to be a characteristic of human brain and mind activity today. Also, they used reasoning to improve their ability to control their natural environment and to control themselves in it, in order to improve their ability to survive and to enjoy life.

For reasons of personal survival, what they were most interested in discovering through reasoning were the relationships between *cause* and *effect* (or effect and cause) in their immediate natural surroundings. Sometimes they were able to succeed, as by recognizing that smashing one rock against another may cause one or both to break into sharp splinters and that these could be used to cut things; that fire causes heat which can warm you but can also burn you; that standing together and using weapons against the leopard drove it away. In these examples they were using what we call "logical" thinking to see actual relationships between cause and effect. But without the evidence about Nature which has since then been acquired they were frequently unable to discover real relationships. When they could not discover a real, natural cause for an event they would simply make up an imaginary, supernatural cause for it which to them seemed to be a logical one, as children do today. We can call that "illogical" or "magical" thinking. Naming things and finding causes for actions and events helped persons to feel less helpless and more in control, whether or not their reasoning was accurate.

Both logical thinking and magical thinking were necessary to human mental development, and they worked together, because magical thinking was able to imagine a cause for an effect which logical thinking was not yet able to. Then, eventually, new evidence would enable logical thinking to provide a natural cause to replace the imagined supernatural cause provided by magical thinking. Thus our early ancestors began to use (without being able to be aware of it) what is called in this book a progressive, balanced, naturally-reasoning, self-correcting, *Human Learning System,* by which the brain and mind could solve persons' problems as these were presented to it, and at the same time advance human thought and knowledge generally by adding logical ideas to the Culture.

In addition to being aware of the non-living things around them, persons were highly aware of the living things and gave them names. By watching animals they learned much from them such as how they hunted, which plants they ate or did not eat, where to find water, etc., and in each case this was logical thinking. However, in order to tell stories about animals they had to ascribe human attributes to them too, which was partly logical and partly illogical (magical) thinking.

A typical example of magical thinking could be that hunters might see a bird in a tree and then find an animal to kill. If this occurred again they might think that the presence of that kind of bird *caused* good hunting, and they would tell the story and people would ask the bird to help them to have success in hunting, and perhaps would wear its molted feathers in their hair.

To consider the next step in our Story, we must recognize that humans had a continuing desire to increase their control over their lives as much as possible. One result of this was for some of them, at some point, to create the idea that everything in their world was controlled by invisible super-humans who lived in a world outside theirs. Their reason for creating this idea was that, although these super-humans were much more powerful than humans, they thought like humans, and therefore could be seduced through praise to give help to humans.

(NOTE: A much later example of this idea of super-humans being in control of everything, including humans, would be the early Greek pantheon in which Zeus was the head God, lived on Mount Olympus, and threw lightning bolts to enforce his reign; Poseidon's lower body was that of a fish, and he carried a trident and lived in and ruled the waters; Aphrodite was the goddess of love and beauty; Artemis, the goddess of the hunt, etc., and people asked their gods for help.)

To continue our Story we need to recognize next that humans were not yet consciously aware of the Human Learning System (HLS), because it was a function of the three brain-system operating below their level of awareness. Nevertheless, it was the *original source* of their ideas, and it continued to function by using information continuously being gained from human studies of the workings of their surrounding natural environment.

Next we need to recognize that the idea of super-humans controlling everything including humans, was introducing a *new source* of ideas for humans, and because it was a manmade idea it was something about which they could be and were consciously aware.

In addition, there were two other vital differences between the old and the new sources of ideas. Because their *original* source continued to focus on the workings of their evolving natural environment, the ideas it created also evolved, and caused the third-brain human Culture to evolve, which was necessary to humans' continuing success (all this unknown to them). At the same time, the ideas created from the *new* source were based only on human imagination and not on the evolving natural environment, and consequently did not evolve. Therefore I assume that to keep their new idea going they formed "praise groups" with leaders. However, as it was a manmade and unnatural idea, and could not evolve, the ideas and Culture it produced became stuck where they were, and stagnated, and became corrupted by power-seeking leaders who kept them alive by *suppressing* new, logical ideas.

The foregoing statements depict my idea of the first wrong change in our course, i.e. the first, lasting human idea to go against the success of The Human Experiment.

The interesting fact is that during this entire time, *all* humans had unknowingly been using the original source of ideas, and continued to, and their ideas and the third-brain Culture continued to evolve beneath everyone's level of awareness.

However, the illogical, *conscious* idea of humans being able to control super-humans who were controlling them was so alluring that it did not die, and, in various forms, still has many followers today. (More on this subject later.)

We will consider "The Second Wrong Change in Our Course" in Chapter 5.

We can see that from their beginning humans have made a specialty of creating ideas and living according to them. It could even be said that our Human Story is of the individual person becoming able to create ideas and share them with others, and of the effects this has had on his and her ability to survive and enjoy life. Some of our ideas have helped us, and some have hurt us. For instance, before our ancestors developed weapons and plans it would have been a hurtful idea for them to try to fight the leopard, and after they developed weapons and plans it was a helpful idea for them to fight it. Crucial questions to keep in mind are: "Which ideas were (and are) helpful and which ideas were (and are) hurtful?" and, "Do we control all of our ideas, or do some of them control us?"

Whatever may prove to be the answers, we can say that humans kept improving their ability to talk and reason, make plans and weapons to defend themselves from predators, and to hunt. Because of these advances, and because their culture included and supported each person in the group, they were able to maintain their new safer and happier way of life, their paradise, for a long time, which was another plus factor toward the success of The Human Experiment.

They used fire for warmth, for cooking meat to make it tender, and to keep predators away at night, which worked especially well when they slept in a cave and put their fire at its entrance.

Learning to use fire was a reasoning and experimental process which required several steps conducted probably over a long period of time.

It began with their coming across a burning piece of branch which had been ignited by a lightning strike. Then they had to overcome their instinctive fear and form the idea of moving close to the burning branch, then form the idea of picking it up by grasping the end which was not burning. Next they had to create the idea of adding fuel to keep the fire going. Then they formed the idea of taking a hot coal with them when they roamed, by containing it in something "fire proof" and later putting it in tinder and blowing on it to make a new fire. Finally someone was perhaps idly pushing a stick into the dirt by rotating it between their palms, and when it was removed they noticed that it had made a hole. Next perhaps they had the idea of rotating the stick into a piece of wood to make a hole and found that the friction caused smoke to appear, so they kept at it until a glowing coal formed which could be used to start a fire. Later someone had the idea of wrapping a leather thong around the fire-stick, tying the thong ends to the ends of a short piece of branch to make a bow, and moving the bow back and forth to make the stick twirl faster. At some point someone noticed that when flint and pyrites are struck together a spark is produced which can be used to start a fire. At some point, another discovery was that using a wooden piston to compress air in a wooden tube (such as bamboo?) produced heat and fire. Ideas for maintaining naturally-created fire, and then for creating it, were more quantum jumps in human thinking and inventing. Thus, through experiment and logical thinking humans gained the use of fire.

For us to have an idea of what their diet may have been we can turn to studies of the !Kung people of Botswana, the so-called bush people of the Kalahari Desert in southern Africa. (The ! in front of the word "Kung" is a pronunciation guide, indicating a clicking sound made with the tongue.) Until a few decades ago they were hunter/gatherers unaffected by the changing world around them. Although they lived in a wasteland that no one else wanted, an arid plateau with only 6 to 9 inches of rain per year, they seldom suffered from lack of food. Some 60 to 80 percent of their diet was of vegetable origin. Their single most important foodstuff was the hard-shelled, protein-rich mongongo nut, but they also ate 84 other vegetables. During the comparatively rainy summer they ate only the fruits, berries and melons they liked best. During the dry season they ate roots, shoots, bulbs and other less tasty though no less nutritious foods. The successful !Kung hunter earned prestige by bringing meat into camp, and a traditional sharing system distributed all of the food to everyone. No one worked regular hours, but a person could gather enough food in 6 hours to feed a family for 3 days. As these people lived this well in a wasteland it seems that the early humans would have lived as well or better, as in their environment plant and animal life were more abundant. An important point is that the !Kung people make decisions collectively with both women and men participating equally in the decision-making process. Perhaps a manifestation of fourth brain function.

Returning to the early people, once they had become able to use fire to cook meat and make it tender their interest in hunting probably increased. Also, cooked meat does not spoil as fast as raw meat. It is important to note that "to hunt" actually meant "to seek, find, and kill," and as their development of weapons improved their ability to do this (i.e. "to hunt") they became more aggressive and more accustomed to killing and to working together quickly as a team to prevent their quarry from escaping. In the beginning they were able to kill only the smaller kinds of animals, but even these were sometimes important to them as food. Gradually they became able to hunt and kill bigger, more dangerous animals. However, successful hunting was (and is) extremely difficult and can require great patience and skill, so usually most of their food came from gathering.

When a group became too large to be sufficiently mobile it continued to be necessary for some persons to form another group, and from time to time groups would meet to renew friendships, exchange news, and for their young persons to find mates. Although they lived in several groups, they continued to think of themselves as being one basic group, one extended family. However as the number of separate groups increased, some moved farther and farther away from their place of origin and from each other in search of food, and over time made changes in their cultural ideas, such as in dress, weapons, habits, language or dialect, religion, etc. When a group met a strange group they would be wary, and might have reacted to them in various ways, perhaps trying to avoid them, or trying to be friendly. One group might have tried to drive off another group to defend an especially good natural food supply, and persons were injured and accidentally or purposely killed, and that was the end of the first human paradise, and a serious setback to The Human Experiment.

However, our Story continued, and during a short period of warming weather 50,000 to 40,000 years ago Homo sapiens hunter\gatherer groups moved north from Africa into southern Europe while ice still covered northern Europe. When cold weather returned, these Homo sapiens, (now known as Cro-Magnons) adapted, not through physical changes as Neanderthals did, but by using their developing mental skills, including to design and sew warm clothing. By 32,000 to 34,000 years ago (by whatever processes) Neanderthals had become extinct, and Cro-Magnons had become the only people of Europe.

Homo sapiens hunter/gatherer groups continued to move northward through Africa, and then out of it and around the eastern end of the Mediterranean Sea into southwestern Asia. From there groups went west, north, or east. The groups which turned west went into the lands of Europe. (Also, there probably was a land bridge from Africa, to Sicily, to Italy which some groups crossed.) The groups which continued northward went into Siberia, and from there some crossed the then-existing land bridge to Alaska and reached North America about 20,000 years ago; some of these found a way through the ice along the west coast and continued southward through North, Central, and South America. The groups which turned eastward went into the lands of Asia, and from there some went southeastward and across the land-bridge of Indonesia, and by water to Australia and then to the islands of the Pacific Ocean. The land-bridges resulted from the drop in water level of the Earth's seas, which occurred because so much water was locked up in the great ice fields and glaciers covering much of the northern surface of our planet.

Remarkably, the rapid expansion of these humans over the planet took place at the climax of the Ice Age, when many parts of the planet were ice-covered. Yet, by their amazing ability to adapt to these severe conditions, human hunters had colonized nearly all of the ice-free parts of the globe by the end of the second Ice Age, 20,000 years ago. As noted, one of their most crucial inventions was the needle and thread, to sew skins together to make warm clothing.

In Europe very early graves have been found in which tools, weapons, and sometimes food had been buried with the body. It seems certain that the relatives and/or friends of the deceased did this as a gift to ease their grief, and/or as a token of respect, and/or the idea had been created that the deceased would go to the "Other World," an afterlife in which these items would be useful. Perhaps the survivors missed their loved one so much that for two reasons they created the idea of an afterlife: so that they could think of the deceased as continuing to be alive, and so that when they themselves died they could join her or him. In any case, we can see that in gaining the higher level of conscious awareness which was so helpful to them, the grim price humans paid was that the individual person became consciously aware of his or her own inevitable death. So through one idea or another they were trying to offset the fear of it, the fear of "the unknown," a fear which still haunts us today.

Around 28 thousand years ago persons got the idea of painting the walls and ceilings of caves. These are found around the world, but the best preserved are in deep limestone caves in south western France and north eastern Spain. Perhaps by creating a picture of an animal a shaman hoped to magically re-create it in the world outside for the hunters to find. Or perhaps they drew and painted as an appeal to the natural forces for protection, or "for art's sake," or to keep records, or for whatever reasons. In any case, it seems that the basic reason for creating pictures was to clarify their thinking, bring it more into their conscious awareness, and share and discuss it with other persons, by making physical representations of their thoughts and ideas. Perhaps this was a manifestation of fourth brain activity.

Chapter 4
The Second Paradise

After leaving Africa a wandering Homo sapiens group came to a region in southwestern Asia north of the Arabian Desert, which today we call "The Fertile Crescent." (It includes parts of what are now Israel, Lebanon, Jordan, and Iraq.) There in the foothills of its northern mountains they found places with plentiful water from rain and streams, and exciting new kinds of animals, fruit and nut trees and bushes, and edible plants, including two kinds of wild grasses (wheat and barley) with seeds at their tops. They ate the seeds, found that they were good food and added them to the other food they obtained from gathering.

Evidence shows that this was the place called "the garden of Eden," and that it was the place about which accounts had been passed down vocally in stories which eventually were written into "Genesis," the first book of the Hebrew Bible (Christian Old Testament), as the story of "Adam and Eve."

Because the supply of food was more varied and plentiful than in any place they had found previously they did not have to move very often or far to find enough to eat. However more food resulted in an increase in the number of persons in the group and soon it had to be divided in two. After a while this dividing became unnecessary because they made a discovery which radically affected the course of our Human Story and led to the creation of the second human paradise: seeds which they had accidentally dropped to the ground had grown there! So they purposely dropped some of the seeds down in new places (and perhaps but not necessarily, covered them with soil to hide them from birds), and when they returned there from gathering and hunting they were delighted to see that the same kinds of grasses had come up with the same kinds of seeds at the top! Therefore they continued to sew more seeds, return later, eat some of the seeds and put others into the soil. (There are other ideas of how food-growing was discovered, but the point is that it was discovered. As written in Genesis, Adam became a "tiller of the soil," and so did their first son, "Cain.") Finally they made the culminating discovery: when the seeds were kept in a dry container they would last for a year or more without spoiling! Being able to preserve food enabled them to stay in one place between harvests and build democratic agricultural villages. Thus the invention of agriculture (controlling their food supply) was another positive factor for The Human Experiment.

Until recently it was thought that agriculture began in well-watered, fertile places such as the Valley of the Nile River in Egypt. However in 1960 Robert J. Braidwood, an archeologist of the University of Chicago, argued that the transition to farming was much less likely to have occurred in a crowded river valley than in some other part of the Near East where climate and other conditions were particularly favorable, such as where humans and wild but domesticable plants and animals existed side by side. As the earliest agricultural settlements then known, those of the Valley of the Nile, were already fairly advanced (dating from around 6,500 years ago), Braidwood conjectured that farming probably originated much earlier than anyone believed. To fill what he thought to be a vital gap between the cave stage and flourishing village-farming communities he proposed to find a transitional village whose inhabitants straddled the borderline between hunting/gathering and farming.

On the hilly flanks of the Zagros mountains in northeastern Iraq, Braidwood found an area and a mound which he thought met his requirements, and he was right. When he and his team dug down into the mound, called *Jarmo*, they found layer under layer, 16 in all, until they reached the original village at the bottom and discovered sickles, seeds, grinders, fire pits, etc. and the outlines of mud houses dating from around 9,000 years ago.

It must have taken 1,000 or 2,000 years before plant and animal domestication reached even such a primitive stage as Jarmo's. That means that before 9,000 years ago humans became able to produce and store food, and that this allowed them to settle where the grasses (cereal grains) grew, build a village, continue to live peacefully together, and continue to develop their democratic form of government. Whereas approximately 250 square miles of land were needed to feed a band of 25 hunter/foragers, six square miles could provide adequate food supplies to the 150 inhabitants of an early farming village.

Outlines of the dwellings of the earliest grain-gathering groups have been found, dating from around 10,000 years ago. These are circles of stones indicating small, round huts which were carry-overs from the nomadic life. The stones apparently reinforced a pole framework that was covered with hides or some other perishable material, and could be taken apart and moved, as were the tepees of the Native North Americans on the western plains. The huts often stood apart from each other with a few paces between them, and were arranged in a circle or oval.

The reasons for this arrangement may be seen by recognizing two features of existing primitive tribal communities in Africa which move from place to place. First, they favor round huts supported by poles, because they are quickly put up and taken down and easy to carry. Second, the biological family, consisting of a husband and wife and their unmarried children, is not always the most important grouping, as it is in most modern societies. The huts are small, and only one man or woman, with or without small children, sleeps in them. Along with a kitchen hut, the sleeping huts are often arranged in a circle or oval with those of the men and women usually on opposite sides no matter who is married to whom. These people are *communalists,* persons with little feeling for personal property and with a strong tradition of sharing. The small huts arranged in a circle without concern for family grouping are an architectural expression of their all-are-equal attitude.

Thus the design of the villages of 10,000 years ago, and of the ones of primitives today, may go back to nomadic hunter/gatherers who, when they first began to gather grains, laid out their first settlements according to plans that reflected their long-established social customs.

As persons began not only to gather but to plant grains, and adapted to sedentary living, they acquired an increasing amount of personal property such as collections of weapons, tools, fuel, clothing, food, and perhaps some livestock, things nomads had not been able to carry with them. More possessions called for bigger houses, and by 9,000 years ago villagers were living in the Jarmo-type of rectangular mud-walled structures divided into apartments with common walls outside and several rooms inside. These apartments had room for an entire family under one roof, plus room for privately-accumulated stocks of food. These two factors weakened the communalist tradition and led parents to think of their families as their first obligation.

Evidence shows that the villagers gathered mushrooms, berries, fruits, and nuts growing nearby, and eventually in addition to grains raised a variety of plants, including peas, chickpeas, lentils, fava beans, onions and muskmelons. Evidence shows that some of the wild animals which lived around them were captured and made tame, i.e. domesticated, and that gave them a whole new steady source of food. The animals domesticated were sheep, goats, pigs and cattle, raised for meat and also for hides which could be scraped and made into clothing, and for milk from cows and goats. (In Genesis, Adam and Eve's second son, "Able," became a "keeper of sheep.") When they harvested the grain they tended to select the largest, healthiest seeds to eat or plant. Every year they again selected and planted the largest, healthiest seeds, so, probably without recognizing it, they were breeding larger and more nutritious seeds through artificial selection, and possibly through accidental crossings of varieties.

Thus the discovery of how to grow and preserve food were further quantum jumps and made possible the creation of the *second human paradise*. In it each person had a great increase in personal freedom from having to search constantly for food, and from being constantly subject to attack by predators, and had more time for enjoyment of life plus the basic sense of personal security that comes from being a needed and important member of a democratic group. Even though they had moved away from being strictly communalists they were cooperative in finding and producing food, building houses, and making and carrying out group plans for cooperative action, and in village life they found the group security and companionship they needed. Also, staying in one place enabled them to have a community fire and take turns in keeping it going.

The men had their traditional duties of hunting, fishing, and making tools and weapons, and they took over the newer occupations required by farming, including the care of the larger animals. At some point, then or later, cattle were used to pull plows to break up the ground for planting. At whatever point in our Story there occurred this change from using human power only to also using animal power, it was another quantum jump. (Horses lived in northern Asia and were domesticated and ridden by nomad herders and brought south later.) The villagers had to be prepared to fight if attacked by a wandering group, but as natural food was plentiful, and their group was becoming increasingly larger, they may not have been attacked. However, a great danger was from fire burning their thatched-roof houses, sparked by natural causes or by human accidents.

The women had their traditional duties of care of children and home, cooking, gathering food such as mushrooms, and finding herbs for flavoring and medicine. Their new occupations included care of the kitchen-garden, grinding grain for cereal and bread, baking, cheese and butter making, basket and pot making, and spinning and weaving.

As persons in the farming village grew older they benefitted greatly from the sedentary lifestyle. Instead of being a burden to a band of roving hunter/gatherers, or having to be left behind, they could continue to participate by being experienced teachers of the village children. Mothers and children benefitted too; a hunter/gatherer mother who is shifting camp can carry only one child, along with her few possessions. She cannot afford to bear or keep her next child until the previous one can walk fast enough to keep up with the group and not hold it back. (Present-day nomadic herders space their children about four years apart by means of sexual abstinence, abortion, infanticide, and lactational amenorrhea, i.e. a woman will continue nursing so as to keep from menstruating so that her seed will not be fertile.)

Unconstrained by problems of carrying young children on treks, village mothers could bear and raise as many children as they could feed. (The birth interval for many farm peoples today is around two years.) The higher birthrate of villagers, together with their ability to feed more people per acre, plus the factor that fewer babies and children were killed by predator animals, let them achieve higher populations than could hunter/gatherers. Older persons and children helped with the household chores, looked after the gentler animals, gathered nuts, berries, and mushrooms, and drove birds away from the crops, and everyone able to participated in planting, watering, and harvesting.

Probably one of the men was especially skilled at helping to settle disputes fairly, and was elected (informally or formally) to be the "chief." However, he was not a dictator. He could call a meeting, and lead the discussions, but decisions were made by the group (probably through consensus). As his job became more time-consuming, at some point it probably was agreed that he had to work only half a day at farming, in order to have time to take care of his official duties, and would receive a half a workday's amount of food from the others. This arrangement was probably applied also to the village shaman, whose task was to appeal to the natural forces for help and guidance, lead the sacred rituals, and help in caring for the sick. Probably he or she had a promising young helper training to take over at his or her infirmity or death.

The formalized human relationship with natural forces, or imaginary gods and goddesses, was the beginning of institutional (organized) religion. Evidence of this found in mounds includes many shrines, figurines of gods and goddesses, and thousands of small clay figurines that seem to have been part of a "Great Mother" cult. Some are made of un-baked clay, and others were baked in accidental fires or, like pots, in an oven or kiln. The most common are of naked women, usually enormously fat, with exaggerated breasts, buttocks, and thighs, and many appear pregnant. The most likely explanation for these figurines is that they were symbols of fertility, and the sculptors' emphasis on features connected with childbearing may have been magic intended to keep the village strong and well populated. Women who wanted children may have received such statuettes from shamans and put them in a shrine, or broken them as a symbolic sacrifice.

(The idea behind these fertility figurines was not new; they bear a strong resemblance to the "Venus" figurines the Cro-Magnons produced some 10,000 years earlier, and the fertility cult was continued from then through the villagers and their descendants down to classical times. As civilizations developed around the shores of the Mediterranean Sea the Great Mother female goddess took a prominent place in almost every pantheon. She was Ishtar in Mesopotamia, Ashtoreth in Canaan, Aphrodite in Greece, and Venus in Rome. The mode of worship of her varied with the desires of her worshipers; sometimes she was the goddess of love rather than of fertility.)

In Halcilar, a Turkish village of about 100 persons some 7,400 years ago, the worship of the Great Mother took an additional form that proved even longer lived. The early stages of this cult are reflected by female figurines that are neither fat nor pregnant, but show a reasonably shaped young woman tenderly holding her child. They symbolize neither procreation nor sex, but motherhood, the underlying idea being to revere or sanctify it.

Not all early Near Eastern villages produced goddess figurines. In fact some offer almost no evidence of religious practices, but it is unlikely that their inhabitants were nonreligious. Primitive people live in a world dominated by powerful and dangerous spirits that must be appeased or won over; they rarely consider it safe to ignore them. So when an early village seems to have had no religion, this probably means only that the traces of its religious activities have not been recognized.

In the mound that was the village of Beidha in Jordan, in all the debris left by some 500 years of occupation some 9,000 years ago, only one Great Mother figurine was found. The village did, however, have something that may have been an austere shrine. About 50 yards east of the village proper were found the remains of three remarkable oval buildings that seem to have been built and rebuilt at different stages of Beidha's existence. The middle building was largest, about 20 by 12 feet, paved with small, angular, deliberately broken bits of stone. When the archeologists unearthed it the floor was unlittered except for a scattering of bone beads. In the center of the building is a standing stone, a great rectangular block of sandstone from the neighboring mountains. This centerpiece is three feet high and positioned so its narrower edges face north and south. Two other slabs of stone were set in the floor, or perhaps raised above it on other stones. Another slab was found outside the building, with the remains of a low stone parapet around it. Nearby was a roughly triangular slab, 12 feet on its longest side and hollowed out to form a shallow basin. Beidhans knew the use of plaster and paint, but the stones were undecorated. The austerity of this shrine-like place and of the image-free holy building of the farmers of Beidha who lived 9,000 years ago is unusual, perhaps even unique, for the time.

It is important to note that from the time humans began making and carrying out plans their sense of personal independence was and continued to be strong, not in spite of their democracy, but because of it, and when they developed the village the chief was a chief among equals. If the people were not satisfied with him they would elect a new one.

(In a recent African tribe, when the people wanted to demote their chief they tipped him out of his official chair. In North America in the Pacific Northwest, if a shaman became destructive it was the duty of his or her relatives to assassinate him or her.)

Because the farmers were growing so much grain and storing it in covered, ventilated granaries which they had invented, they each had some spare time which some persons were using to do other useful inventing. The leather bag had been invented much earlier, and now came the inventions of how to weave flexible twigs or stems into a bag, basket, or hat, make a gourd into a cup or jug, form clay into pots and make them hard in the fire, weave animal hair or plant-fibers into cloth to make clothing, tie or weave strips of leather or stems together to make ropes... which had many uses including to harness cattle... and how to pound certain kinds of pretty "stones" (copper and gold nuggets) into metal shapes for ornaments or knives.

With fire-hardened pottery came also a tremendous improvement in hygiene. Cooking pots could be cleaned easily, and they could be tossed out if they cracked or chipped. Liquids could be stored in vessels and covered with lids to keep out flies and other insects. Clay storage jars kept valuable supplies of grain safe from rodents whose teeth could gnaw through baskets.

So momentous was this great leap forward that many of the gods of the ancient world were likened to potters. The ram-headed Egyptian god Khnum, the creator of all things, was a potter. The Mesopotamian goddess Aruru pinched off a bit of clay to create mankind. The Hebrew prophets, in words that readers of the Bible repeat today, said: "We are the clay, and Thou our potter." Thus, the invention of fire-hardened pottery, and other uses of natural materials including metals, were another quantum jump.

Beneath some 7,500 years of debris, archeologists excavating Tell Hassuna in Iraq uncovered a farming village whose kitchens consisted of two cooking areas, one indoors and one outdoors. In the hot, dry months women prepared and cooked food in airy courtyards equipped with hearths, and in some cases ovens for baking loaves of unleavened bread, and in inclement weather they worked around one or more indoor hearths. The meals prepared in these kitchens represented a radical change in diet, with wheat and barley replacing meat. Fired vessels of pottery served as durable containers for cooking or storing foods and liquids, and enabled cooks to prepare or preserve the harvested grains by boiling, parching, germinating, or fermenting them. Someone discovered that barley seeds left in water fermented and became a slightly intoxicating drink, the original beer, and everyone drank and loved it. Thanks to these inventions women could put together meals that were varied. Served with bread, the main course was likely to be a porridge possibly flavored with chunks of meat, vegetables from the garden, and for dessert there might be nuts or fruit, probably all washed down with barley beer.

Clearly the time of the farming village was one of great creativity, which is what occurs when humans live together in peace, are democratic, and have enough to eat, and out of this burst of creativity there emerged the beginnings of *specialization.* This meant that when persons began to use much of their spare time to make a stone or wooden tool, or leather bag, or leather rope, or metal ornaments or knives, or whatever, they would trade their products for the products of other persons and for food. This trading of things among persons, even among children, had no doubt been going on from the human beginning, but now began to become the economic system called "barter." Increasing specialization, trading, and barter, were another great jump.

Other farming villages had been developing in the foothills in the same or similar ways, so for a long time they were all participants in the second human paradise, and that was a giant move toward the success of The Human Experiment.

Then a crucial problem emerged: the farmers did not know about rotation of fields or crops in order to keep the soil fertile, nor how to add fertilizer to it, so it became increasingly impoverished in such critical elements as nitrogen, potassium, and phosphorous. All of the people in the hills had been practicing what we call "dry farming,"(without irrigation) but even with small irrigation projects, and some accidental fertilizing by droppings of manure by animals, each harvest of grain was becoming less vigorous and nutritious than the previous one. They cultivated new lands, but eventually there was no more unclaimed land to farm. Consequently groups began to fight each other for territory, and that was the end of the second paradise. Periodically persons formed new groups and left, taking their culture, seeds, animals, and farming and manufacturing technologies with them.

Perhaps the creation and development of the democratic agricultural village was an expression of the developing fourth brain, the frontal cortex.

Chapter 5
The Third Paradise and
Second Wrong Change in Course

The departure of the groups which left the farming villages in the foothills of the Fertile Crescent led to the building of new farming villages, and some of these became towns, and some of those became cities. Until recently it was thought that the birth of cities had always been a result of such a progression, from hunter/gatherers, to hunter/ wild-grain gatherers and herders, to the agricultural village, to the development of the town, then the city, and then the development of inter-city trade routes. However, new evidence shows that several cities did not grow from agricultural villages but were established as cities from their very beginning, and that most cities were built long after ancient trade routes had been established, partly, and sometimes entirely, as a result of them.

For example Jericho, located at the southwestern end of the Fertile Crescent, was a city from its beginning and is the oldest city yet discovered; its original wall was constructed around 10,000 years ago, 5,000 years before Sumer's temples and ziggurats and Egypt's pyramids. This original wall was a solid, free-standing structure built of boulders that had to be hauled from a river bed a half mile away and set in place without mortar, and is six feet six inches thick at its base. To find it archaeologists had to dig down 70 feet through the dirt and stone remains of cities and walls built through the centuries, each new one on top of the remains of an older one.

The city covered an area of 10 acres and probably had between 2 and 3 thousand inhabitants. It lay on a natural route of the ancient world, and its people traded with travelers who desired Jericho's manufactured goods, services, and natural resources; the latter included minerals from the nearby Dead Sea, principally salt, highly prized as a preservative, and water that still gushes up from a spring at a thousand gallons a minute. The city dwellers grew their own food, had local sources and also traded for it with travelers. The city was inhabited over a period of some 6,500 years by at least 10 different cultures, during which time it appears to have been destroyed one or more times by earthquakes and rebuilt each time. Human habitation of the city ended with the Biblical Battle of Jericho around 3,500 years ago, but any traces of the walls Joshua is reputed to have sent tumbling down have been erased by erosion. The modern city of Jericho is a cluster of lush parks, palm trees, and attractive homes, surrounded by the great expanse of the desert. It lies next to the 50 foot high mound which contains the remains of the ancient city.

The region around the Tigris and Euphrates Rivers came to be called *Mesopotamia*, a Greek name which means "between the rivers." Some of the groups which left the farming villages in the northern foothills of the Fertile Crescent moved southeast into Mesopotamia, which forms the southeastern part of the Fertile Crescent, and built small farming villages in the two river valleys. Each spring the two rivers overflowed and left coarse-textured silt, a highly productive soil, so farmers no longer had the problem of the fertility of the soil becoming depleted (and moved to higher ground when the annual floods came). The annual rainfall was inadequate, but that was not a problem because after the flood the fields could be irrigated from the rivers; thus, farming on naturally-fertilized land was another quantum jump. The villagers continued to have their traditional strong sense of personal independence and democracy, the chief continued to be elected and to arbitrate but not rule, and was a chief among equals: thus was created the *third human paradise.*

As the farmers from the north settled along the rivers, they encountered groups already living in the marshes and cane brakes. These people were hunting/gathering/fishing groups, and on the plain farther away from the rivers roamed nomadic herders. We do not know what occurred when the farmers encountered these non-farming groups, as there is no known record.

We do know that where the waters of the two rivers joined before going into the Persian Gulf, the annual overflow had created a very large delta region. Eventually farmers coming from the north arrived there and found that non-farming humans had been living there for some time, obtaining their food from the marshes and cane brakes, including plants (fruits, berries, greens, etc.), fish, waterfowl, and other animals. Excavations indicate that when the farmers from the north reached the delta, among the groups living there they may have encountered a group of persons called *Ubaidians,* who like themselves were non-Semitic-language-speaking persons. It seems that these people had been able to plan and cooperate sufficiently to dig ditches and drain some of the marshes and swamps to have solid ground, and had built villages and temples. It is possible that the farmers from the north may have assimilated with these people and that, as the delta was annually re-fertilized by the overflow of the rivers, together they built a great number of farming villages and became the *Sumerians.* (The origins of the name Sumer and of the Sumerian language are not known.) In any case, the farmers from the north did build farming villages there.

Between floods the farmland had to be irrigated; building and maintaining permanent irrigation systems, both to reach existing farmland and to create new farmland, required organization, in order not only to dig the ditches but to keep them open of accumulating silt. The already-elected village chiefs who had worked only half-time in agriculture in order to have enough time to settle general disputes among persons, perhaps were asked to expand their duties to include full-time managing of the irrigation system, and to settling disputes about the allocation of land and water, etc., and received additional food in compensation.

In conjunction with the farming operation, some persons continued to use some or all of their time specializing as craft persons, and bartered their wares for food, skins, and other items; money had not yet been invented. After the invention of the potter's wheel its use also became a specialized craft, and eventually everyone was some kind of specialist, including the farmer, the herder, the fisherman, and the craftsman, and was involved in bartering with everyone for everything. Some villages had raw materials and/or finished products that others lacked, so inter-village trade and barter were begun. At first they did not have stones or metal to work with as these were not to be found in the silt-covered areas, but eventually all necessary raw materials were brought in from other areas by traders, and were bartered for.

A major step which the villagers took was to expand their ideas for using animals for power and transportation. Although oxen were able to pull plows, they were too slow to be used as pack animals, so eventually wild asses (donkeys) were captured, domesticated and used to carry things and eventually to bear a rider. (Sometime later camels were domesticated and used in the same ways.)

The process of development was that one village in a group of villages would grow larger than the others and become a town. Then between 5,500 and 3,800 years ago several of these towns grew to become the great city-states which together comprised the region called *Sumer* (not Sumeria), known as the world's first *civilization*. It was a social movement so inventive and powerful that it led 2,000 years of our Human Story and left a legacy that reaches down to the present time. Therefore we will give it considerable attention.

The word "civilization" comes from the Latin *civis*, meaning "citizen of a city." Thus, civilization means a way of life advanced enough to include living in cities. "Advanced" means having specialists, i.e. farmers, herders, fishermen, and hunters who produce enough food to support persons who do not produce food. Some of the latter furnish manufactured goods, and others furnish services including government, religion, education, medicine, and police/military protection. Required also are math systems, writing, laws, and an accompanying form of culture.

In the Sumerian civilization the first, richest, and largest city, Uruk (called Erech in the Bible, and Warka in modern Arabic), had some 45,000 inhabitants at its height around 4,800 years ago. It had broad avenues lined with date palms, large palaces, towering temples and pyramid-like ziggurats, and grand, two-story, balconied houses of the wealthy. Other notable Sumerian cities included Umma, Lagash, Nippur, Eridu, Kish, Sippar, Adab, Larsa, Eshnunna, Shaduppum, Isin, Jemdet, Nasr, Shuruppak, Mari, and Ur. Sumerian buildings were made of sun-dried brick because there was no stone and little wood. Sumer's cities had division of labor, monumental building, organized religion, and satellite agricultural villages providing food including barley, dates, wheat, many kinds of vegetables and meats, and superb, slightly intoxicating, barley beer. Sumerians took part in the invention of writing and of the wheel, helped to develop the oldest known mathematics, and developed the world's first written law code. The story of Sumer is of vital importance to us today, because its rise and fall became a model of what has occurred since then. Understanding its story helps us to see why we have the opportunity to "break the mold" today.

Our knowledge of the Sumerians comes from excavations made by teams of archaeologists from several nations. By digging carefully into ancient mounds they found not only the remains of streets, buildings, houses and domestic life, but found thousands of clay tablets, the earliest written records of our Human Story. Thus the Sumerians had made a critical quantum jump: they had learned to write. From representational picture writing they had evolved into the creation of the abstract system of writing called *cuneiform*, which employed wedge-shaped symbols made by pushing a wedge-shaped stick into soft clay tablets. These were then allowed to dry, or baked, to become permanent records which report on all subjects of daily life in the villages, towns, and cities of Sumer. What we know about the daily lives of the Sumerians is revealed in the thousands of clay tablets which have been found in the ruins of their cities, and laboriously translated by scholars into modern languages.

Also found were numerous small stone cylinders. Before the development of writing, Sumerians indicated personal ownership by carving a design into a cylinder, which was then rolled across a wet clay tablet, making an imprint of the design. Many of these signature designs used religious or mythological themes.

Probably an early step toward a village growing to become a town would have been the creation of a central market place. This probably would have occurred in the original village (or in a newer one if it were more central and/or larger) which had several intersecting paths connecting it to the villages around it. Perhaps the pattern was for growers to find a place to set up stalls for food, such as fresh fruits and vegetables, dates, beans, apples, onions, garlic, turnips, and sometimes dried fish, pork, and duck. Then a specialist, say a maker of stone tools, set up his shop next to the food stalls. Then a metal worker came, and perhaps a potter opened his shop near the others. Then a weaver came, and an artist who sculpted or modeled figurines symbolic of gods and other subjects. Probably there were street musicians, singers, dancers, acrobats, storytellers, magicians, and other performers. More and more persons in the town and from the surrounding villages were attracted to the market area for the convenience of being able to find several things in one location and to barter one kind of goods for another, and/or for the excitement of the crowd and the entertainment.

Sometimes specialists would have a surplus of sheepskins, sacks of grain, pots, copper or gold jewelry, or other items that they had taken in trade, so a merchant would set up a store (a "trading post" or "general store") next to the other specialists and take whatever surplus they had in exchange for whatever supplies they needed, and people came to trade with him too. Then other specialists came, some from other villages, and set up their businesses there, so a central market place was created, and people came from the villages to shop, and sometimes to stay, and the central village became a town.

In the process the village had grown not only in size but in the sophistication of its inhabitants. The merchants and other specialists had done daily bartering, and this sharpened their wits and improved their ability to acquire a surplus of goods. Then they could use these to pay carpenters to build large homes for them to live in, and pay weavers to make fine robes for them to wear, and pay other persons to perform other services, including big, well-armed guards to protect the merchants' caravans from being raided by nomads, and to protect the merchants' homes and businesses from thieves.

This was another disastrous turning point in our Human Story, because what the persons who acquired a surplus of goods learned was that they no longer had to treat others with respect in order to get their help. Previously, getting help had required involving others in a democratic plan of cooperative action, but now people could *hire* persons to help them, including bodyguards. On the surface of it there was nothing wrong with hiring persons. This was neither illegal nor against the town's morality of the time. It was no longer a custom to share food or goods, so one could acquire a surplus and do with it whatever one chose to. From the standpoint of the person acquiring and using a surplus, he or she was only pursuing the human goal of each person to continually improve his or her ability to survive and enjoy life. Today, of course, we often hire other persons to help us do things, but we have contracts, laws, constitutions, bills of rights, and courts to protect persons and democracy. However, at that time these safeguards did not exist, and consequently accumulating a surplus and using it to hire others led to the breakdown of democracy and to the fall of the third human paradise.

At that time humans were not consciously aware of "democracy" as a form of government, even though they had created and lived successfully in it for millenniums. They were totally unaware of their actual Human Story, and of the Human Experiment, and could not know that one's only real way to pursue the human goal successfully was to participate in creating and carrying out group plans of cooperative action. One could not know that in acquiring and using a surplus one was initiating a trend which led to a, perhaps the, disastrous turning point in our Human Story, including in The Human Experiment.

This brings us to the importance of the point made in Chapter 3, that in the human beginning, rather than competing with each other to create a hierarchy of *individuals* within their group, as animals do instinctively in order to dominate each other, people used their human brains, minds, vocal language, and reason, to consciously create a cultural hierarchy of *ideas* within their group, so as to minimize instinctive competition and maximize their instinctive human proclivity to work together, in order to dominate the animals *around* them.

Without knowing it the persons who began hiring other persons had stepped backward in human development and were creating an *animalistic* hierarchy of individual persons. In it, by using a surplus one could become a personality which was neither animal nor human, a personality which could think, reason, and make and carry out complex plans of personal action, and thereby become more powerful and cunning than any animal, but no longer truly "human" because it was not dedicated to making plans with others democratically.

This human tragedy occurred because the surplus led to a division in the creation of wealth which led to a *ruling class,* which reversed the ideas and goals of the human social structure and culture and ended the third paradise by destroying six of its essential elements: the ideas of personal equality, liberty and responsibility; the ideas of democracy, morality, and the opportunity for all persons to attain the human goal (i.e. to continually improve his/her ability to survive and enjoy being alive). This destruction was caused by the persons in "The Establishment" (i.e. persons in authoritarian positions such as governmental, business, religious, educational, police or military, etc.) who consciously and purposely *suppressed new ideas* because they liked the way things were and did not want change.

The devastating consequence of preventing new, logical ideas from replacing old magical ideas was that it not only injured the progressive balance in the Human Learning System, but went beyond that by twisting its positive effect into a negative effect. The result was that the individual person was stopped from growing, stopped from maturing, stopped from evolving, stopped from moving toward the human goal.

We can recall the background for this tragedy as being that sometimes the early humans were able to use logical thinking to see actual relationships, but were frequently unable to. When they could not discover a real, natural cause for an event they would simply make up an imaginary, supernatural cause for it which to them seemed to be a logical one, as children do today. We have called that "illogical" or "magical" thinking. Both types of thinking were necessary to human mental development, because magical thinking was able to fill the gap which logical thinking was not yet able to. Then, eventually, new evidence would enable logical thinking to provide a natural cause ro replace the imagined supernatural cause provided by magical thinking. Thus our early ancestors invented a progressive, balanced thinking system, which served the person during his/her life span, and advanced human thought and knowledge for future human use: a crucially important step for everyone toward democracy.

When the members of The Establishment suppressed new ideas and relied on old ones it halted the development of the thinking system and stagnated the Culture, putting the human brain and person into a mental cage. Also it invited increasing tyranny. Hence, for the second time in our Human Story, and in the course of our Human Experiment, there had come into being an anti-human, anti-democracy power group, and instead of being consciously considered a needed and important member of human society, the individual person had become expendable.

To see the depth of what occurred we can go back to the early humans. Through their ability to use vocal language and to develop conscious cooperation they built a special, protected place for themselves to be in within the surrounding natural environment. This place was composed of their cultural ideas, the basic one of which was that each person was a needed and important member of the group, i.e. that each person was "in." This special place was not a cage, but a haven and "launch pad," because the cultural ideas were continually being improved in favor of each person, by each person, through the democratic creativity of the community. However, this special place of ideas could continue to exist only as long as humans kept the necessary ideas alive. When they stopped doing so in Sumer the special place ceased to exist, and there was no longer an "in" for anyone to enter into. This was a devastating blow to all persons, especially to children, for the following reasons.

While they are growing up, and their brains, minds, and bodies are developing, children are completely dependent on older persons. For this reason they need to think that the older persons are completely competent to protect them, have a master plan for everyone, and comprise a magic group that the child wants desperately to become a part of, so that he/she will be safe. We call these older persons "authority figures," or "survival figures." We can hardly overestimate the importance of the role which these figures play in the mental and emotional development of children. They sense that over them these persons hold the power of life and death. Because of their feeling of total dependency on these persons, children are enormously sensitive to the persons' attitudes and behavior toward them. The children seek the persons' attention and acceptance and fear their indifference and rejection.

While children were growing up in the pre-agricultural groups, because they were accepted and helped by the members of their group they were automatically "in." In the first agricultural groups it was the same for them, and as village life became more complex, and the learning period grew longer, they were still not disappointed, because when they became of age they were accepted into the group through rites of passage.

However, after the creation of the town and city-state there was less and less a viable "in" for children to be accepted into, and in some cases none. This alone was bad enough for the children, but there was something even worse. Because children had of necessity formed the idea of their survival figures being able to accomplish anything, the children had to assume that the adults could accept them in if they chose to, so the children had to assume that they were purposely being kept "out."

The terrible result was that, because of their feeling of total dependency, children could not allow themselves to think that there was anything wrong with their survival figures, so they were forced to think that there was something terribly wrong with themselves. Also, especially in certain cases, each one thought that he/she was the only one being kept out. No one had enough information to recognize that the new Culture had rejected *everyone*. Thus, human society went from being a situation in which everyone was "in," to becoming a situation in which, for one reason or another, everyone was "out." This can help to explain why people became angry, jealous, cynical, and overly ambitious: "the lonely crowd."

With a growth in commerce money was invented in the form of metal coins, and the surplus goods could be exchanged for it. That made it easier to set values on goods and labor, and easier for the traders and merchants to obtain, store, and use personal wealth. From then on, to and including the present time, there have been six main *manmade* forces guiding humans: the desire to secure their sources of food and other natural resources; the need to recover from the feeling of being "out;" the continuing effort to discover the secrets of our surrounding natural environment; the continuing creation of human forms of government and the attempts to make them work; sexuality (even though the urge for sexual intercourse is natural, the human exploitation of it has too often made sexuality a cruel, destructive, unnatural, commercial obscenity); and the acquisition and use of money, this last because it can give one all of the material comforts of life, plus *power*, which in this case means power over other persons, whether the power be economic, political, religious, domestic, military, parental, sexual, or other, and can also seem to be a way of getting "in" socially.

As we have seen in our own time, power over other persons is something no one can handle. As the historian Lord Acton famously observed, "All power tends to corrupt, and absolute power corrupts absolutely." Once persons are put into positions of power, it is almost impossible for them to give them up. The need for power becomes a disease; the more power the afflicted persons acquire, the more power they feel they must have if they are not to perish. They feel they must be able to do whatever they desire to do whenever they desire to do it. They feel that they need more material things, a bigger house, more servants, more political influence, and so on.

This situation pleases no one. The persons in power are not happy, because they are hated and afraid of being robbed, kidnaped, or assassinated by their rivals or by the people. They live in a constant state of fear and denial, blinding themselves to their cruelty by dehumanizing their victims and then despising them. In doing so they dehumanize themselves and become even more cruel. Their interest is only in what they think will be advantageous for themselves. The persons not in power are not happy, because they are angry at being forced to obey the dictates of their masters whether or not these are reasonable and/or just, and are ashamed of not being in control of their personal lives.

As we know today, the human brain is an intricate and complex organ, and this radical cultural shift caused it great confusion. During the time of the villages, humans had retained the basic group bonds and customs that had given them social stability and had helped them to get along with each other and to cooperate. Now these were broken, and one could no longer be sure whom one could or could not trust.

Thus the new Sumerian Culture did not represent or meet the basic human desires or needs of anyone. It was a "dark" culture, and makes us realize that by comparison what they had been enjoying during the three paradises was a "bright" culture. In it persons in groups were motivated to help and keep each other up, but in the dark culture they were motivated to help and keep themselves up by keeping the others down. Whereas the bright culture was an accepting and inclusive one, the dark culture became a rejecting and exclusive one. The dark culture continues to exist today and to reject everyone. This is the basic cause of persons being unhappy and angry, without knowing the cause of their unhappiness and anger. The result is that they blame each other for their unhappiness and anger, and this creates a horrendously miserable situation.

What occurred specifically in Sumer is that as the town had grown larger, the town's chief had also been acquiring goods and property, and expanding his organizing power, and becoming more important not only in the town but outside it, while the chiefs in the surrounding villages were becoming less important. Thus the farmers were losing their traditional independence of government, and democracy was failing not only in the town but in the villages. However, the villagers knew of nothing they could do to prevent this shift, and it did bring them two important benefits.

One benefit was personal protection, brought in the following way. Beyond the farming villages lived nomad herders who drove their sheep and goats from one patch of green to the next and brushed against or clashed with the farmers from time to time. If a bad year dried up water holes and scorched the pastures, some nomads were driven to attack the farming villages. The town's chief and town council had hired a permanent body of armed men to act as police (or soldiers) to guard the town and keep the peace by using the tribute (taxes) paid to them by the town people. Because the villagers had become increasingly important to the towns for food, the chief sent the soldiers to protect them (and subsequently to collect taxes from them).

The second benefit came out of the necessity to enlarge and improve the irrigation system to serve the farmers. This required many men, and the centralized authority of the town was able to organize them and to manage the work. This expanded workforce made canals long and wide enough to carry considerable bodies of water, not only to irrigate farmland but to drain swamp areas and create more farmland.

Even with the increased protection some villagers desired the safety of a larger, better organized place to live in, so they drifted toward the walled towns that were growing into walled cities. For example around 5,000 years ago there were 146 villages surrounding the central village of Uruk. By 4,700 years ago so many of them had been incorporated into Uruk that their number had dwindled to 76 and Uruk had become a town. In the 300 years that followed their number shrank to 24 and Uruk had become a city-state. During the same period the number of cities, at this time meaning settled areas of more than 100 acres, grew from 2 to 4 to 8.

We can see that food production was essential not only to the creation of the second and third paradises, but to the emergence of the non-food-producing specialists in the towns and cities, including politicians, priests, and other bureaucrats. Hunting/gathering societies had tended to be egalitarian, lack full-time bureaucrats and hereditary chiefs, and have small-scale political and religious organization at the level of the group or tribe, because almost all persons were engaged in acquiring food. Once food could be grown and stockpiled, a city's or town's political and religious elite could assert the right of taxation, escape the need to produce its own food, and engage full-time in political and religious activities through which they were gradually building a pyramid of power with themselves at the top.

Before looking further at the rise of cities we need to recall that while the farming villages were rising in the foothills, the earlier-imagined gods of the gathering/hunting groups became imagined gods who were thought to control not only human affairs but the growth or failure of crops and animals. Consequently people believed it absolutely necessary to hold protective ceremonies to honor the deities and be in their favor, so each foothill and valley village had a shaman, who in the town became a more worldly "priest," to lead the ceremonies and honor the deities by making offerings and sacrifices to them.

As the culture became less and less inclusive of all persons, the feeling of being "out" grew, and people turned increasingly to religion as a way of feeling "in." Religion became so important in Sumerian life that by the time of the cities there were hierarchies of priests in them and temples had become major elements. At first they were community property, built and maintained as offerings to the gods who represented the forces of nature upon which life depended. The temples were seen as being the gods' houses, and to them persons brought offerings of food, pottery, and sometimes figurines or ornaments.

As food became more plentiful, the cities' temples became repositories and redistribution centers for it, also serving as sanctuaries to the refugee, sources of relief to the needy, and major employers of workers. Soon after 5,000 years ago a temple in the city of Lagash had a daily ration list for beer and bread for 1,200 men and women, of whom 300 were slaves. It ran a cloth workshop employing 205 women and their children as carders, spinners, and weavers. It had bakers, millers, brewers, and cooks. It also employed fishermen, herdsmen, sailors, guards, scribes, blacksmiths, and many other workers. The temple also mounted its own land and sea expeditions to bring back items such as precious stones, metals, limestone for the temple foundations, and timber for the temples and for the balconies around the second stories of the houses of the wealthy. It was in order to keep track of the temples' activities that the Sumerians learned to do arithmetic and to write in cuneiform.

Just as important as personal safety was the city's promise of personal fulfillment, because a variety of roles awaited the man and woman there. In fact the city depended not only on numbers but on variety, and its concentration of numbers was possible only because its residents performed specialized duties that would be supported by the larger society. No longer was every man forced to be a hunter or a farmer, nor every woman a mother and housekeeper. From the time of the very first cities workers were needed to manufacture trade goods, conduct trades, tend shrines, do nursing and mid-wifing, build houses, create art, drive donkeys, undertake massive construction projects, and so on. The exciting variety of city life, offering the possibility of following a personal bent rather than a parent's footsteps, must have been as powerful a lure 5,000 years ago as it is today.

The family had always been the foundation of the Sumerian social structure; it was monogamous and patriarchal, and property was handed down from father to son. Women were respected and had the right to own property, possibly inherited from their husbands or relatives.

As life in the cities developed there occurred a loosening of the family ties and tribal responsibilities that had been so important in the early groups and villages, and replacing them were ties to craft and responsibilities to the city. Each craftsman belonged to a craft group, and each craft was identified either by its occupation or by the name of some animal, such as the snake or ram. The craft group members' responsibilities to the city went beyond their jobs as sculptors, painters, masons, gardeners, carpenters, potters, weavers, bakers, butchers, metal smiths and the like. If there was a crisis at an irrigation dam, for instance, they could be called up as a unit and dispatched to make emergency repairs. They could also be called to help with the harvest. If an enemy attacked a city, or if a city wanted to attack an enemy, the craftsmen were conscripted and each craft group was put under the command of its foreman. Several platoons constituted a military company which was headed by an officer, and for these services the men were paid in food, clothing, or money. *In this way the first standing armies were created.*

Women were primarily wives and mothers, and still respected as such, and records show that some women were engaged on their own in international trade. Some women and children were employed by the temples, and by wealthy persons as household servants, and probably were assistants in crafts and worked in market places. Women slaves could be used by their owners for sexual acts, and some free women may have been driven by poverty into prostitution. Most children's education came from their parents, but also there were organized schools for boys to become scribes. The writing system was extremely difficult to learn, requiring years of schooling, as by 5,500 years ago the written vocabulary of Uruk contained 2,000 different signs. (An alphabet had not yet been invented.) However, success at it ensured a position among the upper classes and lifetime employment. In addition to their professional duties some of the scribes began to write narratives expressing their feelings, such as complaining about their masters, telling about arguments with fellow scribes (sometimes ridiculing each other), composing poems, and so on, using clay tablets to write on: the beginning of literature.

The persons in the city were descended from families which had been village farmers and had left the farms and gone to the cities to enter the crafts and professions. Some of these persons still owned the family land either independently or together with several members of their families. By 5,000 years ago much of the land had been purchased in large segments by wealthy aristocrats and by the priesthood for the temples' holdings. By 4,800 years ago the temples still owned a good deal of land, but a large part was held by groups of wealthy citizens who bought and sold land as *syndicates and corporations.*

In the city-states community decisions were made by unelected, self-appointed city councils of wealthy, aristocratic elders and priests. When the need arose for military defense or offense the city council chose a member to function as a temporary king for the duration of the emergency, who afterward would return to his own affairs. As populations grew and cities expanded they fought each other increasingly for land and water rights, and this fighting between *independent, politically-organized, city-states with armies was the beginning of the insanity we call "war."* The intervals of peace grew shorter and shorter, so the kings ruled for longer and longer periods of time, all the while growing more powerful, and by 2,800 years ago kings had superseded the elders and were in control of the cities. However, the temple kept its firm grip on the people, so the king always sought the blessing and support of the priests in his conduct of worldly affairs. At the same time, the priests kept the right to help appoint the king or to approve the elders' choice, and the king in turn became head priest. He enlarged and beautified the temples as a means of increasing his stature in the eyes of his subjects and of the gods. The next step was for the kingship to become a hereditary monarchy. *Thus were born, in Uruk and the other cities of Sumer, three ideas that would influence human history for thousands of years: the military and political unit which was the city-state; war; and the divine right of kings.*

We can see that one reason why it was easy for the slide to occur from democracy to an elite, to kings, to king/gods, was that children had been taught about the gods and goddesses as being powerful, magical figures upon whom they depended and whom therefore they must fear, worship, and obey. As a result of this, when traders and priests in the cities acquired power, controlled the government, and hired soldiers, people had already been conditioned to fear, worship, and obey power, so they continued to.

Even today we tend to be impressed by persons with high rank, and by "the lifestyles of the rich and famous." We can imagine how the common people felt when they were shoved back against buildings lining a street to let pass noble persons reclining on litters carried by slaves, the nobles dressed in richly colored robes and wearing jewels and golden crowns, and all being surrounded by large, fierce armed guards.

Thus in Sumer the cities had become the perfect settings for the creation of tyrannical hierarchies of powerful persons who claimed to be in touch with the gods, and eventually claimed even to be gods themselves, and that was why the third paradise collapsed so quickly. Adults had set themselves and their children up to become cogs in a nonhuman, anti-person machine, and had then let themselves be used to be slaughtered when one city machine was pitted against another through the horror of war.

Next after kings, priests, and nobles in Uruk's hierarchy were the rich people, the big landowners and merchants who owned the fleets of ships that carried on extensive sea trade with places as far distant as Bahrain in the Persian Gulf, the Indus Valley cities of Mohenjo-Daro and Harappa, and Egypt. Next were the lower bureaucrats and tradesmen, then sailors, farmers, fishermen, and water carriers, some employed by the temples, some by the secular aristocracy, and at the bottom were slaves.

Slaves were a late development in Sumerian cities, but their number grew after 5,000 years ago when there were several large cities on the Mesopotamian plain and there was intense strife among them. Most slaves must have been prisoners captured in battle, for in Sumerian the word for "slave" derives from the word for "foreigner." Other slaves had been impoverished nomads or marginal farmers who sold themselves and their families in bondage to the aristocrats or to the temple, in return for a roof, meals, and the security of the city's walls.

There may never have been great numbers of slaves in Uruk itself, but their work was important to city life. They were most often in weaving workshops, bakeries, the temple complexes, the kings' palaces, and the households of the privileged classes. According to the records they were mostly women, but it is not certain what was done with male captives. They may have been organized into labor gangs for the military and listed in the records in a category other than slave, or they may have been considered too dangerous, and killed.

Some of the unearthed clay tablets show that the Sumerians imagined a past in which people lived in a god-created paradise. This was expressed in a poetic tale that described the conflict between the king of Uruk and the distant town of Arrata, the earliest known description in writing of a paradise and the fall of humankind. The poem describes a period when there were no creatures that threatened people: no snakes, scorpions, hyenas, or lions, a period in which humans knew no terror. There was no confusion among various peoples speaking different languages, with everyone praising the god Enlil. Then something happened that enraged Enki, the god of wisdom and water, who had organized the earth in accordance with a general plan laid down by Enlil. Enki had found some sort of inappropriate behavior among humans and decided to put an end to the Golden Age. In place of it came conflict, wars and a confusion of languages (as in the story of the Tower of Babel).

Also there is the story of Gilgamesh. One of the oldest epics in world literature, it is a collection of ancient folklore, tales, and myths that gradually developed into a single work. To summarize it very briefly, it centers around Gilgamesh, a powerful king of Uruk, half human and half god, about 4,700 years ago. He was a terror of a king, a man who chased girls, slaughtered wild beasts, pursued real or imagined enemies all over the country, and so upset his subjects that they appealed to the gods for help against him. In response the sky-god Anu creates the wild-man, Enkidu, to meet Gilgamesh in combat. After a mighty battle Enkidu and Gilgamesh become friends and share many adventures, until Enkidu is caused to die by the gods as punishment for his and Gilgamesh's having killed the Bull of Heaven. As he is dying, Enkidu describes the Netherworld to Gilgamesh. He sets out to avoid Enkidu's fate and makes a perilous journey to visit Utnapishtim and his wife in the hope of gaining immortality. They had been granted it by the gods and were the only humans to have survived the Great Flood. Along the way he encounters the alewife Siduri who attempts unsuccessfully to dissuade him from his quest. He completes his journey by punting across the Waters of Death with Urshanabi, the ferryman.

Gilgamesh meets Utnapishtim who tells him that the gods had decided that humans were evil and so created a great flood to drown them. He said the gods told him in advance of it to build a huge boat to preserve vegetation and "the seed of humanity." It had rained for seven days and seven nights and his boat was "tossed about by the windstorms on the great waters." When the storm subsided the sun god Uta came forward and shed light on heaven and earth. The boat went aground on the top of a mountain and Utnapishtim opened a window and let in light from Uta and sent out messenger birds. Then he prostrated himself before Uta and sacrificed an ox and a sheep. Finally he and "the seed of all living things" had found a home in the land between the two rivers.

He tells Gilgamesh that if he can stay awake for 6 days and 7 nights he will become immortal, but he falls asleep. When he wakes, Utnapishtim decides to tell him that if he can obtain a certain plant from the bottom of the sea he will become young again. He obtains the plant, but does not eat it immediately because he wants to share it with the other elders of Uruk. He places the plant on the shore of a lake and while he bathes it is stolen by a snake. Gilgamesh returns to Uruk where the sight of its massive walls motivates him to praise this enduring work of mortal men. He sees that the way mortals can achieve immortality is through lasting works of civilization and culture.

According to the Greek scholar Ioannis Kordatos there is a large number of parallel verses as well as themes or episodes which indicate a substantial influence of the Epic of Gilgamesh on the *Odyssey*, the Greek epic poem ascribed to the poet Homer. Thus the story of Gilgamesh foreshadowed not only the Biblical story of Noah, but also the wanderings of Odysseus and Hercules. The tale was written down first in Sumerian, then in Akkadian, Hittite and, in one variation or another, eventually in almost all the languages of the Near East.

The Sumerian kings built palaces that rivaled even the monumental pyramid-like ziggurats in area. One king's palace erected in the city of Mari covered more than eight and a half acres and its central courtyard was paved with precious alabaster. Other courts had frescoes portraying deities and the kings' military exploits. Some palaces had as many as 300 rooms for the family, court officials, guards, servants, and guests. When kings died their tombs were filled with exquisite bowls and other vessels of silver and gold, cult figures of lapis lazuli, and gold daggers of exquisite artistry. Before 5,000 years ago Sumerians had discovered how to combine tin and copper to make bronze, and weapons made of it were found. Also found were decorative figurines of animals, carts and chariots, and ceramic jewelry whose beauty went unequaled for centuries.

In death the Sumerian kings were as self-centered as in life. From the royal tombs of Ur have come not only objects of art but also the remains of full-size ceremonial chariots complete with the remains of oxen, soldiers, guards, musicians, and dignitaries of the court. While still alive they were drugged and then entombed along with their dead rulers. Human sacrifice was an established feature of the last rites for a monarch; one tomb yielded 74 members of the royal retinue who went to the grave with the king, presumably to be handy for service in an afterlife. Perhaps a king believed that he was being generous to the ones who were entombed with him, as they were getting a free ride with him to an afterlife. Still, he could have asked.

The variety of populous life produced differing opinions. Sumerian scribes complained, and one wrote that he was a "thoroughbred steed" but pulling a cart carrying "reeds and stubble." Another complained in writing of the stupidity in one city taking enemy lands and then the enemy coming and taking them back. Rather than merely complaining, people in the city of Lagash instigated history's first recorded revolt. This came after Lagash's rulers had increased local taxes and restricted personal freedoms. Also, Lagash's bureaucrats had grown in wealth, and the people resented these affronts enough to overthrow their king and bring to power a god-fearing, law-respecting king named Urukagina, who eliminated excessive taxation and rid the city of usurers, thieves, and murderers: the first-known reforms.

As the use of writing increased in Sumer, businessmen wrote down their transactions. Sometimes these were later used to settle disputes and eventually the accumulated actions, along with the laws which had been passed down by word of mouth, were made into a written code by Ur-Nammu, a Sumerian king who reigned about 4,100 years ago. His code predates by more than 300 years the code of Hammurabi, a king of Babylon who about 3,750 years ago set down a series of minutely detailed laws that was long believed to have been the first law code in the world, and it predates the Ten Commandments by almost 1,000 years. In Ur-Nammu's code the penalties were enlightened, generally prescribing fines instead of physical punishment. The fines were paid in silver shekels and silver minas, which shows that money had come into use by then.

Common Sumerians remained illiterate, and though they were once the electorate, they had lost their power completely and become subject to tyranny. The monarch was viewed as an agent of and responsible to the gods, and it was the religious duty of his subjects to accept his rule as a part of the plan of the gods. Common people were obliged to pay taxes to the government in the form of a percentage of their crops, which the city could either trade away or use to feed its soldiers and the others it supported. Thus out of a division in the creation of wealth came personal power and a new human plan by which government passed from the villagers to a chief in the town, to an elite in the city, to a dictator/king, who became a hereditary monarch.

It could be said that the third human paradise was officially over when the persons in the Sumerian villages lost democratic government and the traditional independence they had enjoyed through it. From the human beginning up to this loss of democracy and personal freedom, except for some setbacks which were always overcome, people had been moving gradually toward attainment of the human goal of each person to continuously improve his or her ability to survive and enjoy life through participating in creating and carrying out group plans of cooperative action.

During the time of the Sumerian elites the insanity called war was invented and cities fought each other. Instead of being inspired by their leaders to work together, people were forced to kill each other, and to kill prisoners or make them slaves. The victims were not only those who were killed or disabled or enslaved, but the ones who were forced to commit these wretched acts. Killing or disabling or enslaving others is wrenching to the human mind and spirit.

However, it is important to recognize that during the two thousand years of Sumerian activity persons had opportunities to open their minds in ways which are necessary for democracy today. One way was that the city offered the opportunity for a person to think of new possibilities for personal fulfillment. Four other ways resulted from the invention of writing:

– Laws were put into writing, and that led eventually to crucial elements such as courts of law, the English Magna Carta, the Declaration of Independence by the American Colonies, the Constitution of the USA, and the Charter of the United Nations Organization (UN).

– Laws had been passed down vocally from generation to generation,
and it was believed that they had been made by the gods and
could not be changed. When Sumerians began to put the laws
into writing their intended purpose was to standardize and
clarify them, but as they did they generalized them, and added
to them, and began to realize that new laws were being created
by themselves, not by their gods.
– Scribes began to write complaints, poems, hymns, proverbs, essays,
and epics, the beginning of written literature, some of which led
to modern democracy.
– Clay tablets tell us the history of the changes in the social structure,
what succeeded and what failed, and we can benefit from this
experience.

Thus the new way of life in towns and cities affected all aspects of
human thought and activity and became the pattern for all that followed,
even to the present time.

The Sumerians were a mixture of peoples and ethnicities and, as noted,
the origin of their language is not known, but it was non-Semitic. While
Sumer was growing, peoples moved into Mesopotamia, probably from
the west, and adopted much of the Sumerian culture, but they spoke
Akkadian, a Semitic language similar to Arabic and Hebrew. Because
the Sumerian cities fought each other they were vulnerable to attack
from outside. During this fighting, in an obscure city in northern
Mesopotamia an Akkadian-speaking man named *Sargon* rose to power
and gave the city the name of Akkad. Starting around 4,300 years ago
as King Sargon the First, he conquered all of Sumer, then extended his
empire both eastward and westward, and ruled for 61 years. It would
seem that his people were still bonded by tribal customs and loyalties
which could inspire them to be a formidable fighting force. Under
Sargon the Akkadian language displaced the older Sumerian language,
but he caused the Sumerian city-states to stop making war on each other,
and united them.

At this point in our Human Story we need to ask ourselves some vital
questions: What had happened to the Human Experiment? Had it proved
to be too difficult for humans to make it succeed? Obviously, we were
no longer creating new survival ideas which were helping all persons to

better survive and enjoy life. Is it inevitable that the necessary new ideas we need will continue to be suppressed by our letting the acquisition of money and personal power be our guide to our thinking and acting?

We shall see that it is too early in our Story for us to know the answers to these questions, and that there is much more to be learned, beginning with the following chapter.

Chapter 6
The Aegean Civilizations

It is important to note that as cultures advanced and spread, the peoples of various regions exchanged ideas and inventions and intermarried. This mingling of cultures and peoples occurred through commerce, conquest, and migration. Traders carried the products of one culture to others over long land and sea routes of commerce, and the soldiers of conquering armies often settled in lands far from their own. Also large groups of people migrated from one region to another, brought the customs of their homelands with them, and many adopted the ways of life of the people they joined. In this way the developing cultures of the world continuously mingled, a striking example of which occurred in the region of the Aegean Sea.

We can begin this part of our Human Story by noting that until little more than a century ago the history of the Western World was thought to have begun with Classical Greece and ancient Rome. No one dreamed that the epic poems of the 9th Century B.C. by the Greek poet Homer were more than myth. That began to change when a self-made, wealthy German businessman named Heinrich Schliemann, who had read Homer's *Iliad* many times, decided that it was not only legend, but also a literal historical document.

Born into poverty in rural Germany, Schliemann signed on as a ship's boy for a passage to Venezuela. The voyage had just begun when the ship was wrecked and he was cast up, naked and nearly frozen to death, on the shore of Holland. After several years and various jobs, he began doing important work for a Dutch dealer in commodities, and at age 25 he set up his own business. Of the many books he read, the one which fascinated him was the *Iliad,* and having by age 40 acquired a large personal fortune, in 1868 he decided to retire from business and search for the ruins of the ancient city called "Troy."

Having once been married disastrously to a Russian, he wrote the Archbishop of Athens, an old friend, and, having set out the qualifications a good wife should have, requested that one be found for him. The Archbishop came up with a striking-looking 17 year-old Greek village girl, Sophia Engastromenos. Schliemann married her and, surprisingly, the union was a great success. He worshiped Sophia, and trusted her completely, the only human being other than himself he did trust. She was devoted to him, and to her delight he took her with him to help him on his archeological expeditions.

He decided to search along the northern shore of the Aegean Sea, today the seacoast of modern Turkey, just south of the Dardanelles (ancient name Hellespont), where long tradition said Troy had been located. (Troy was called *Ilios* by the Greeks, hence the title of Homer's poem, the *Iliad.*) There were two earth mounds to choose from, each one several acres in size, marking the sites of two ancient cities. The experts said that if there were a Troy around there it was probably the site farther inland. Schliemann did not agree. He reasoned that if, as the *Iliad* said, the Greek invaders were forever trotting back and forth between Troy and their camp on the seashore, making several trips a day, Troy had to be the site nearer the water. He made contact with the British man who owned half of the site (named *Hissarlik*) and, not bothering to inform the Turkish owners of the other half, he organized a force of local workmen and began to dig. Without realizing it, he found not one, but nine Troys, layered one over another. At the bottom layers he found ruined walls of immense stone blocks, broken pottery, spear tips, stone weapons, huge clay jars as tall as a man, and much evidence of fire and destruction. He thought he had found the ruins of King Priam's palace and Priam's treasure: a hoard of silver vases and knives, gold diadems (head bands worn by royalty), earrings, and more than 6,000 gold rings and buttons. In later years the layer he thought was Homeric (Troy II, next to the bottom) turned out to be far older, dating from before 2000 B.C. In his feverish search for gold, Schliemann had dug right down through what is now conceded to have been Homeric Troy (Troy VII, dating from about 1250 B.C.). Nevertheless, he proved that there had been a Greek civilization long before that of the people who had been thought of as the "ancient" Greeks of the classical period, and he proved that the Homeric Troy had actually existed. (We now have evidence showing that early Troy was founded as a Phrygian city, with a culture dating from before 2000 B.C. The Trojan War may have reflected a real war over control by

Troy of trade through the Dardanelles, the strait connecting the Aegean Sea and the Black Sea.)

Schliemann next turned his attention to Mycenae, on the "Peloponnesus," the large peninsula forming the southern part of the Greek mainland, where there was a ruined citadel. The remains of a fortified city from the remote past, its walls had been built of huge stones even larger than were found at Troy. Throughout Greek Classical literature Mycenae had been associated with the Greek side of the Trojan legend, whose heroes had sailed off to fight at Troy under Agamemnon's leadership. He was, according to Classical lore, the king of Mycenae, the richest and most powerful ruler in Greece. Schliemann dug again, and unbelievably again struck gold. Within the walls of Mycenae he found five royal grave sites containing a number of skeletons and stuffed with incredible hoards of gold and bronze objects of all kinds, including bronze swords for fighting. He assumed that he had found the grave and gold of King Agamemnon, but modern archeology has shown that these discoveries belonged to an earlier age, perhaps hundreds of years before Agamemnon was born.

Even so Schliemann and his young bride Sophia had found the home of the Mycenaean Greeks, the people whose famous legendary warriors such as Achilles and Ajax attacked the city of Troy in about 1250 B.C., and after a long siege conquered it by hiding some soldiers in the famous wooden horse. The Trojans brought it into the city, and that night the Greek soldiers crept out and opened the gates to their army. But the poet Homer (or Homers, there may have been several) did not sing about this war and the exploits of its legendary heroes in the *Iliad* and the *Odyssey* until some 500 years later, basing his knowledge on legends and myths which had been memorized and passed down from person to person, sometimes father to son, sometimes by palace minstrels, none of whom could read or write. Stories about the war probably began as short tales of isolated events and heroes; eventually a profession of story-telling was established and these new "bards" began combining the stories into larger narratives. (We have evidence of bards memorizing the complete poem word for word, over 25,000 lines of poetry. A group would gather for an evening's entertainment and a bard would begin to sing the stories. Eventually it required many such evenings to tell all of them).

Schliemann went next to the island of Crete, the large Mediterranean island at the southern end of the Aegean, where there were reputed to be ruins of palaces even larger than at Mycenae. However, after a quarrel with the owner of a site (Knossos) about the number of olive trees included in the sale, he broke off negotiations and did not investigate the site. Afterward archaeologists made excavations there, and in all the Aegean Sea region, and found that an entire, previously unknown, Aegean civilization had developed there from 3000 to 1100 B.C.

The story began when reliable ships were developed and people ventured into the Aegean Sea from somewhere to the east as early as 7000 B.C. It is not known whether they came from Anatolia (now Turkey-in-Asia), or from the highlands of Persia, or from the Black or Caspian Seas; in any case some of them built elaborate cultures into civilizations, first on the small Cycladic Islands dotting the Aegean Sea, and then on the island of Crete. The people who settled there were traders who built their civilization, called *Minoan* after the legendary King Minos, on the ideas and inventions of Egypt and the Middle East. Excavations on Crete have found the remains of very impressive palaces and works of art, including at Knossos and other places, dating from around 1700 B.C. The palace at Knossos was excavated and beautifully restored by a dedicated archaeologist named Arthur Evans, who made it his life's work. He found many staircases, halls, rooms, storage vaults, bathrooms, and even separate drainage systems in each of its sections to accommodate the torrential rains that fall on Crete in the autumn and spring.

Although Crete is mountainous, it had large, rich valleys, forests, vineyards and olive groves. The Minoans learned to write sometime after 2000 B.C., and left specimens of their writing, but it is yet to be deciphered. However, according to their beautiful fresco paintings in the palaces, and their superb sculptures, the Minoans were preoccupied with sports (including leaping over the horns of bulls), sunny religious practices, processions and dancing, the beauties of the natural world, and at the same time hardworking and prosperous, gifted architects, able craftsmen, shrewd traders, experienced sailors, and good fighters with a large fleet of ships. Their manufactured goods went everywhere, and they eliminated piracy in the Aegean. By 1700 B.C. the Minoans had become dominant in the area. A question is, why did they not fight among themselves? The answer may be that after about 2000 B.C. fairly dense populations were beginning to concentrate around 5 or 6 main power centers. These were just beginning to emerge as palace complexes and were due for an enormous growth in size and opulence over the next 300 years. The largest of the palaces was at Knossos, but there was another of impressive size and wealth at Mallia not far away, and an even more luxurious one at Phaistos on the south coast, across the island from Knossos.

Apparently the reason why these groups did not try to conquer each other is that something new occurred in the Aegean world: "palace economies" emerged, grew larger, and ultimately became the pivots around which all Minoan society revolved. Everything that went on in a Minoan state probably was directed from the palace: great hoards of oil and grain were stored there; the impetus for the arts was centered there; crafts flourished there; wealth was concentrated there; all favor and privilege were dispensed from there. Who was redistributing and dispensing is not known, whether the palace occupants were kings, queens, high priests or whatever.

If all the palaces on the island were considered to be parts of a very large redistributive system, its parts interlocking to the mutual benefit of all, the redistributive system itself, in its developed palace form, could have been a deterrent to warfare, because there would have been no incentive for the states to fight each other. Clearly the Minoans were a people of great vigor, originality, and wealth, and lived on Crete for a very long time, indicating success for the Human Experiment.

The origin of the other famous people who came into the Aegean Region, the Greeks, also is not known, but it is clear that they were Indo-European. They, or their ancestors, may also have appeared in the Aegean region as early as 7000 B.C., and mingled with the aboriginal Stone Age hunter/gathers on the mainland of what is now Greece. If that is so, then the language and the people that would later be known as Greek evolved there. A contrary view holds that the original Greeks were intruders who appeared from the east shortly before 2000 B.C. In that case, the newcomers probably spoke a language that was proto-Greek.

Thus there was a Greek civilization long before Homer, and long before Troy. It can be called *Helladic*, because that is the name given to the entire cultural sequence that came out of the Stone Age on the Greek peninsula, flowered there, and expired in about 1100 B.C. The name Mycenaean applies only to the last phase of Helladic culture, a period that ran from about 1600 to about 1100 B.C.

Greece is a mountainous land unsuited to growing grains, and the early Greeks were uninspired subsistence farmers until they found that there was a large market for their olive oil and wine, began to trade these for food and other goods, became aware of riches in other places, and became ambitious. They were the people called the Mycenaean Greeks, after their city of Mycenae. Between about 1600 and 1100 B.C. they traded with the peoples in the small Cycladic Islands and with Crete. Eventually the Mycenaeans occupied them, and penetrated east to the island of Rhodes and the cities of Miletus and Ephesus on the coast of Anatolia (now Turkey in Asia). These Mycenaean Greeks became powerful and wealthy. Like its Minoan model, a Mycenaean palace was a combination military and administrative center, manufacturing plant and warehouse.

For example the palace of Pylos specialized in pottery, much of which went up the west coast of Greece and over to Italy and Sicily. At the time Pylos was destroyed (about 1200 B.C.) it had a stock of 2853 stemmed drinking cups stacked in one room alone. It was a hive of activity, capable of making everything it needed, from harnesses to armor, including a quantity of extra things for export. The tablets found at Pylos make clear the wide variety of specialists working in the palace. They catalogue the output of these craftsmen, keep detailed inventories, note how much of this went to one man, how much of that came from another, record allotments to be paid out by the palace and taxes due in. Careful records were kept of everything, down to a notation about two oxen named Glossy and Blackie. Troops were ordered about, and a close check kept on military supplies.

The subsidiary towns in the domain— secondary collecting points for woven cloth, lumber, or farm products— were necessary not only for the economic functioning of the whole enterprise, but were also dependent on the palace for their own protection and for the supplies of raw metal or clay, or whatever key commodity they needed for their work. Something like bronze would have been doled out to them by the palace, as they did not have access to such materials directly. The palace – its port, its fleet, its soldier-traders who went voyaging and dealt with foreigners– had such access, and in that way kept its own people tied to it. They could not function without the palace, and the palace could not prosper and be strong without them. It levied troops from them, armed them, trained them, and led them in battle.

There had been an enormous volcanic eruption on the Aegean island of Thera about 1500 B.C. (which caused the center of the island to sink under water, resulting in the supposedly mythical "lost city of Atlantis" which was erroneously described by Plato as having been in the Atlantic Ocean). Up to that time the Minoans were clearly the dominant influence in the Aegean, but the Mycenaeans were pushing out, becoming trade-oriented and expansionist-minded. Their experience as seamen was growing, and they were beginning to learn where the best markets and the best sources of raw materials were and going directly to them. They seem to have done this in harmony with the Minoans, perhaps even with their assistance.

But growing economies and growing populations need larger and larger bases. Since Mycenae and Crete were both expanding, it was inevitable that at some point they would collide. When the collision came, Crete was so ravaged economically and politically by the indirect consequences of the Thera eruption that she was no match for the Mycenaeans when they moved in, and she more or less abdicated control of the Aegean and capitulated to them without a struggle. The Mycenaeans had no wish to destroy the Minoan palace system. They wanted to manage it themselves, clear away the executive deadwood at the top and put its assets to work as part of a larger and richer enterprise of their own, and they established their headquarters at Knossos.

For an unknown reason the other Minoan palaces and the large, luxurious villas all over Crete were destroyed. Equally mysterious is the final destruction of the palace at Knossos in about 1380 B.C. Whatever the case, the destruction of Knossos does not mean a Greek departure from Crete; Mycenaeans of some type stayed on. Homer lists Idomeneus,

King of Crete, as one of the commanders who came to Troy to fight. He commanded 80 ships and was described as the ruler of "Crete of the hundred cities.."and he was a Mycenaean.

During the 14th Century B.C. the Aegean Sea became a Mycenaean lake, as the mainland palace-states continued to push their ships into all its corners and beyond. Wealth poured in and the population mushroomed. Of all the mainland palace-states, Mycenae grew the fastest, and by 1300 B.C. it was the most important place in Greece. However, beginning shortly before 1200 B.C. in a series of holocausts the great Mycenaean palaces were destroyed. For a long time the damage was thought to have been done by the Dorian Greeks coming from the north between 1100 and 950 B.C., but this was not the case.

The background is that there were large populations in all the palace-states, and a humming mercantilism dependent on placid foreign markets to soak up Mycenaean products in exchange for large supplies of food. Only if that two-way trade could continue could the Mycenaean palaces continue, but this trade could not continue, because the eastern Aegean was in turmoil. This was greatly because in 1288 B.C. the Egyptians under Pharaoh Ramses II went north with a great army to crush the Hittites and regain control of the land along the Syrian and Lebanese coasts, and the two armies met in a gigantic battle. In addition there emerged another force destructive to trade. As neither the Egyptians nor the Hittites were seagoing empires, they recruited navies from those who were. This resulted in the emergence of the so-called "Sea Peoples," who were active in the eastern Mediterranean and the Aegean in the last half of the 13th Century B.C. They seem to have been confederations of coastal and island peoples, taking advantage of the big struggles on land to engage in organized piracy. Ugarit, most cosmopolitan of the Levantine (eastern shores of the Mediterranean Sea) ports was sacked and burned at the end of the 13th Century B.C., presumably by a mass attack by the Sea Peoples. Piracy had become a way of life in both the Eastern Mediterranean and in Ionia (an ancient region on the west coast of Asia Minor and on adjacent islands in the Aegean Sea).

The bad news of the destruction of trade began to be evident as early as 1250 B.C. (and as in all societies, before they could begin to understand what was about to happen to them). There must have been disturbing pileups of export goods, food shortages, unemployment, and great civil discontent. Ambitious dynasts are certain to have taken advantage of the situation and begun chopping away at the control of established kings.

This state of affairs began showing up with increasing clarity in Greek myth, in stories like "The Seven against Thebes," in which a small group of heroes tried to drive a corrupt ruling dynasty from a powerful walled city. That legend is now given historical weight by the knowledge that Thebes was sacked sometime between 1250 and 1200 B.C. After Thebes the other palace-states fell like dominoes:

- Pylos, sacked and burned just before 1200 B.C., apparently a victim of an overwhelming piratical raid.
- Gla, a fortified town on an outcrop of land rising from a drained lake bed just north of Thebes, demolished by unknown hands.
- Iolkos, farther north in Thesslay, sacked and burned some time between 1200 and 1150 B.C.
- Tiryns, near Mycenae, sacked and burned probably after 1200 B.C.
- Mycenae, attacked before1200 B.C. and all the houses outside the citadel walls destroyed; attacked again just after 1200 B.C. with evidence of further destruction, the citadel itself breached and the palace attacked some 70 years later.
- Smaller places all over Greece, poorly garrisoned, feebly walled, if walled at all, went up like kindling and vanished.

Thus, it seems that the Mycenaean civilization was destroyed by those involved in this time of chaos, including Sea Peoples and the Mycenaeans themselves, which chaos made it easy for the Dorians to come in, and they too may have done some of the destroying.

In any case, by about 1100 B.C. Mycenaean culture had disappeared. It was replaced by a feudal society of great poverty and much violence, and the population plummeted. The survivors holed up in crags secure both from the dangerous sea and from their equally dangerous neighbors. Artists, having no royal patrons to serve, lost their skills, grew old, died, and nobody replaced them. Similarly with the great masters of pottery and metalwork. No records were kept, and ultimately the abilities to read and write were lost, along with everything else. This is called the Dark Age of Greece, and it lasted for three or four hundred years.

It was during this time that the stories of the Trojan War were created and passed from person to person. The *Iliad* is the story of an event in the ninth year of the war (which was said to have lasted ten years); the great hero Achilles is offended when the leader of the Greeks, Agamemnon, takes a slave girl Achilles has been awarded. Achilles withdraws from the battle and prays to his mother, Thetis, a goddess, to turn the tide of battle against the Greeks. The Gods grant Achilles his prayer, and he does not return to battle until his best friend is killed by the great Trojan hero Hector. Achilles throws himself into the battle, fights Hector, and kills him. In a final gesture of contempt, he ties Hector's lifeless body behind his chariot and drags it around the walls of Troy.

If there is a theme to the epic it is "Achilles' Choice." He has been offered the choice either to be a great and famous hero in war and die young, or to live a long, happy life without any lasting fame whatsoever. Although Achilles initially chooses not to die young, the death of his friend forces him to make the choice that will make him famous for all time, but tragically dead at a young age when an arrow strikes him in the heel, his one vulnerable spot.

The *Odyssey* is the story of the homecoming of another of the great Greek heroes at Troy, Odysseus. Unlike Achilles, Odysseus is not famous for his great strength or bravery, but for his ability to deceive and trick. (It was his idea to put the soldiers into the wooden horse.) His homecoming has been delayed for ten years because of the anger of the gods; finally he is allowed to go home. For most of the ten years he has been living on an island with the goddess Kalypso, who is madly in love with him. He too is offered a choice: he may live on the island with Kalypso and be immortal like the gods, or he may return to his wife and his country and be mortal. He chooses to return to his wife and be mortal, and much of the rest of the work is a long exposition on what it means to be "mortal." If the Odyssey has a discernable theme it is the nature of mortal life, and why any human being would, if offered the chance to be a god, still choose to be mortal. The Greeks in general regard Homer's two epics as the highest cultural achievement of their people, the defining moment in Greek culture which set the basic Greek character in stone. Throughout antiquity, both in Greece and Rome, everything tended to be compared to these two works.

As noted, between 1100 and 950 B.C. the Dorian Greeks, who were illiterate and far less advanced culturally than the Mycenaeans, came from the northwest part of Greece down into mainland Greece, and eventually they overran most of the Peloponnesus and the entire western half of Crete. The Greeks descended from them and from the Ionian Greeks (another group of immigrants) called themselves *Hellenes*, their Greek homeland was known as *Hellas*, and they were the Greeks who created the famous classic period from 750 to 338 B.C. which is called the *Hellenic Age,* the "Golden Age of Greece." During it Greek culture reached great heights of development in such city-states as Athens, Corinth, Sparta, and Thebes, and Greek armies and traders colonized many areas along the Mediterranean and Black Seas spreading their culture as they went. The Greek position was that anyone who was not Greek, or perhaps did not speak Greek, was a "barbarian,"(from the word meaning "foreign country," hence, a foreigner.) The Romans applied this term to anyone outside their Empire, or who perhaps did not speak Latin.

By 500 B.C. the belief of the Greeks that they inhabited an island of freedom in a sea of despotism was well founded. By then the monarchies and aristocracies of heroic Greece had faded away in most places to leave a world comparatively little marked by variations of wealth and privilege. Its free citizens were accustomed to ruling their own lives, and, except in Sparta, many slaves differed little from them in the pattern of their everyday lives, the structure of their families, and the range of their occupations. The Greeks began to express a sense of community when they came together for festivals of games and music (the Olympiads probably from 776 B.C., and at the shrines of the most famous oracles), and many of them joined together to defeat the Persians. As Greece expanded, Xerxes I, ruler of the powerful Persian Empire, had tried to take over Greece and its colonies. The Greeks were strong, highly disciplined soldiers and sailors, and though greatly outnumbered a long war ended with the defeat of the Persians in 479 B.C.

The plays, the histories, the philosophy of the golden age which followed are marked by an intense curiosity about the nature of human beings as social animals, possessed of the power to shape their destiny and thereby obliged to define and seek "the good." For example, Pericles, the greatest of their leaders, said to his fellow citizens, "We Athenians, in our own persons, take our decisions on policy and submit them for proper discussion; we give our obedience to those whom we ourselves put in positions of authority." Thus they believed not only in the idea of the need for government, but in the idea that it should be a product of the participation of the governed. Athens became the leading city, and from 461 to 431 B.C. magnificent buildings were constructed and great works of art and literature were produced. Also, the Greeks made great advances in theater, government, and philosophy, which in Greek means "love of wisdom."

The earliest people that we have records of had theories of the beginning and nature of things, and they wove these ideas into their religion.

Western philosophy dates from 600 B.C. when the Greeks turned to inquiry independent of religious creed. As the earliest known philosophers, i.e. thinkers interested in the nature of the Universe, they asked themselves: What is the stuff from which all things in the universe come?

Thales, who lived in Miletus in ancient Greece about 600 B.C., was the first to propose a solution. He said that water was the original stuff. He saw water turning into solid ice when it was made cold, and into air and steam when heated. Therefore he reasoned that everything from the hardest rock to the lightest air, originally came from water and in the end returned to water.

Anaximander, another citizen of Miletus, said that the original stuff was not water, but a living mass which filled all space; he called this mass "the infinite." In the beginning it was whole, not broken into pieces, but it contained motion, which caused it to move up and down, back and forth, and around. Slowly pieces were broken off from the mass so that eventually all the things that we have in the universe came into being. As the motion continued, these innumerable pieces would be brought back together and the mass would assume its original identity.

Anaximines, a third thinker from Miletus, proposed air, because of its attribute of infinity, which would account for the varieties of nature.

These three philosophers of Miletus were followed by a group of philosophers who, although they were interested in the same problem, were more interested in finding out the many ways in which the many things in the universe were related. These were the *Pythagoreans,* a group or school founded by Pythagoras. They were impressed by the fact that many things could be stated by numbers. For example, the tone of a wire or a piece of gut is related to its length in a manner which can be expressed in numbers. So, they reasoned, numbers must be the stuff for which philosophers were looking. (Hence I see these philosophers as returning to the early humans' studies of the relationships between cause and effect, or effect and cause, in the workings of their natural environment, which became the Human Learning System, and eventually the scientific Method.)

Classical philosophy (Greek and Roman) emphasized a concern not only in the ultimate nature of reality, the nature of the Universe and its basic components, but with the problem of *virtue* in a political context. However practically all of the problems of philosophy were defined by the Greeks eventually, most notably by Socrates, Plato, and Aristotle.

Socrates, one of the greatest of the Greek philosophers, was born and lived in Athens from 469 to 399 B.C. His interest was in solving human problems, and his guiding rule was "know thyself." He believed that goodness in a person is based on knowledge, and that wickedness is based on ignorance: no knowledgeable person would deliberately choose what was bad for him or her in the long run, but most persons, through ignorance, may choose an evil which appears to be good at the time. He found that people in Athens held many different opinions about what is good or bad, and he realized that these opinions had not been tested to sift out knowledge. He knew that gaining knowledge of how to lead a good life is not a matter of teaching a few rules, but is a lifelong process. He taught by questioning his students about their opinions, then asking them further questions about their answers and having them respond. This process helped them to develop their minds, learn to think for themselves, and go beyond opinion and search out truth. (This is known as "the Socratic Method.") He was a loyal Athenian citizen and brave soldier, but his methods finally offended several important people in the city. They made up charges that he tried to introduce new gods and was corrupting the youth of Athens. At his trial he defended himself in a speech which Plato, one of his students who also became a great philosopher, described in his famous work, the "Apology." Socrates was found guilty and condemned to death by drinking a cup of Hemlock, a poison which causes one to suffer terribly while dying. He could easily have escaped from Athens, but chose to follow the laws of the democracy and, with several of his friends around him in his prison cell, he kept his convictions even to death, and emptied the cup.

Thus, Socrates' life reflected his ethical views, and was entirely devoted to seeking truth and goodness. He lived simply, and could share equally well in a luxurious banquet with his wealthy friends, or endure the hardships of a military campaign. On one occasion he walked barefoot through the snow without seeming to mind. He was always loyal to the democratic form of government at Athens and during his lifetime had the courage to stand up for his convictions. Twice he defied the government in power, risking his own life in the name of justice for others. He was married and had several children.

The quest for the highest good, to which the actions of free men should be directed, is ideally depicted in the dialogues of *Plato* (428-347 B.C.).

The results of calm enquiry into the nature of the visible world are set out in the writings of his pupil *Aristotle* (384-322) of Stagira, an ancient town in NE Greece. Aristotle's works, surviving in effect as lecture notes collected by his pupils, cover every branch of the knowledge of his time, from aesthetics and politics to botany and physics. Their conclusions dominated western thought for more than 2000 years and their method still does. He made close and dispassionate observations of diligently collected facts, from which conclusions are drawn with scrupulous attention to the soundness of argument and the legitimacy of deduction, without any appeal to the supernatural to resolve the mysteries of nature. Because of his strict attention to factual evidence, Aristotle is known as the "father of reason," and he has taught us to take reason for granted. Nor did this reason defeat itself by resting on instinct. Its basis in the nature of language and knowledge themselves was examined and set forth in his logical works, which remain the foundation of all rational thought.

Other lasting achievements are in the area of art, especially Greek sculptures such as the Venus de Milo, and in the areas of theory, especially mathematics and physics. The work of Euclid (around 300 B.C.) and Archimedes (around 287-212 B.C.) in these fields was not surpassed until the age of Descartes and Newton.

As previously noted, the Greeks created their famous pantheon of gods who they believed lived on Mount Olympus. Zeus, the chief god, ruled the other gods and goddesses, who were all related to him. The main gods were Apollo, god of light, music, and youth, Dionysus, of wine, Pluto, of the underworld, Hephaestus, of fire, Hermes, of flocks and travelers, and Poseidon, of the sea. The main goddesses included Hera, the wife of Zeus, who was goddess of marriage and birth, Aphrodite, of love and beauty, Artemis, of hunting, Athena, of war and wisdom, and Demeter, of crops. A legend said that Zeus came down from Mount Olympus in the form of a swan and seduced Leda, who gave birth to the beautiful Helen, whose abduction by Paris of Troy from her husband Menelaus, king of Sparta, was the cause of the Trojan War. Hence the famous saying that Helen's was "the face that launched a thousand ships." (The war was actually a huge piratical raid by the Greeks around 1250 B.C.)

Most Greeks believed their gods were superhuman beings friendly to them. They felt that they could anger the gods only by impiety or insolence. In contrast to other ancient peoples the Greeks did not live in terror of their gods, and held many festivals in their honor. The programs included dramas, prayers, animal sacrifices, and athletic contests including the Olympic Games held every four years. They had high regard for healing shrines, such as the one at Epidaurus, and their Oracles interpreted the will of the gods in temples at Delos, Delphi, and Dodona.

Eventually, however, Greek religion seemed almost as childish as fairy tales to many thoughtful Greeks. In about the 330's B.C. they turned first to philosophy and then to various Oriental religions for spiritual aid and comfort. Isis, an Egyptian goddess, and Mithras, a Persian god, attracted many followers. Some were attracted to popular "mystery cult" religions which abounded in the Mediterranean lands. The "mystery" applied to a mystical, symbolic union with a god who lived in human form, died, but came back to life again. Through a secret ceremony that symbolically united them with the god, the believers were assured that they could change their human nature to divine nature and thus gain a happy afterlife. There were a number of mystery cults, with different gods, but all of them emphasized the salvation resulting from dedication to a dying-rising Lord. This idea may date back to the early agriculturists who associated their lives, gods, and many rituals with the birth, life, death, and rebirth of plants.

In the political traditions of the West the beginnings of the idea of democracy are associated with the city-states of Greece. As noted, the word itself is derived from the Greek *demokratia*, from *demos*, "the people," and *kratos*, "rule," thus, *rule by the people.*

In its original meaning, democracy is a form of government where the right to make political decisions is exercised directly by all of the persons of age in a community acting under procedures of majority rule or consensus. This is known as *direct democracy.*

It is one of the most obvious and natural ways of organizing a community, and, as we have seen, it began with early humans. Today it continues to be found in primitive societies and in some modern communities.

In the Greek city-states direct democracy was possible because of the limited number of persons participating. Only certain qualified males were considered citizens, and only citizens could vote. The city-state was small, and women and slaves were not citizens and not allowed to vote. In fact, Greek democracy was possible only because the large number of slaves permitted the necessary leisure for the male citizens to devote themselves to public affairs. They recognized the equality of citizens, but failed to develop a general concept of the equality of all persons.

The Greek version of direct democracy was widespread in Greece, especially during the 5th Century B.C. All citizens were entitled to attend the legislative assembly and to vote, and to run for office. However, their inability to develop a system of *representative democracy* kept them from creating large democratic states. (In representative democracy the citizens exercise the same right not in person but through representatives chosen by and responsible to them. *Constitutional* democracy is a form of government, usually a representative democracy, where the powers of the majority are exercised within a framework of constitutional restraints designed to guarantee the minority certain individual or collective rights, such as freedom of speech and religion.)

The government of Athens went through many changes in democratic forms, the best-known being one based on a constitution worked out by the Athenian statesman Cleisthenes in 508 B.C. He saw that the existing system of tribes in Athens, with their constituent units of *phratries* (brotherhoods) and clans, worked against the effective functioning of democracy. This was because the divisions of phratry and clan, having not only blood and religious associations but also associations of property, caused local and family interests to predominate in the four existing tribes and enabled noble families to exert undue influence in politics. To remedy this undemocratic situation, for voting purposes Cleisthenes abolished the four tribes and created ten new ones on an entirely different basis.

First, he divided Attica (the region surrounding Athens) into three new districts: urban (including suburban), inland, and maritime. Next, he subdivided each new district into ten geographical areas. Finally, he created each of the new tribes by taking one new geographical area from each of the three new districts. The result was ten new, smaller tribes, each one of which included people from all parts of Attica, so that electoral divisions ceased to be identical with those of clan and property. Also he made it possible for more persons to qualify for citizenship. This new organization was for political purposes only. For religious purposes the clans and phratries retained their old signification.

The names of the new tribes were taken from legendary heroes and therefore contributed to the idea of a national unity. Each tribe had its shrine and its particular hero cult, which was free from local association and the dominance of particular families. This national idea Cleisthenes further emphasized by setting up in the market place at Athens a statue of each tribal hero.

One novel part of the new constitution was that a prominent citizen who threatened the stability of the state could be banished by a vote of *ostracism,* without any charge being brought against him, but he did not lose his citizenship. Any citizen entitled to vote in the assembly could write a citizen's name on a shard (a fragment, usually of broken earthenware). Either 6,000 votes had to be cast and the man with the majority was ostracized, or at least 6,000 votes had to be cast against a particular man, it is not known which. The ostracized man had to leave Attica within 10 days, and stay in exile for 10 years, but he remained owner of his property.

The Athenians were the first people to try to form a democratic federation, a league of free cities united under Athenian leadership in common devotion to the democratic way of life. Unfortunately, during this time there was a struggle for domination between democratic and oligarchic states, of which Athens and Sparta were the representative examples. (An oligarchy is a form of government in which power is vested in a few persons or in a dominant class or clique.) Envy of Athens by Sparta and other Greek city-states led to the Peloponnesian War, 431 to 404 B.C. During the war voluntary cooperation in the democratic federation broke down, and the experiment ended with the victory of Sparta.

After the defeat of Athens the victorious city-states quarreled among themselves until 338 B.C., when they were conquered by invaders from their northern Greek neighbor, Macedonia, led by King Philip II. His son, Alexander the Great, became the ruler of Greece and expanded his empire throughout the Middle East and Egypt, and as far east as northern India. Under Alexander's successors Greek culture continued to spread and to combine with other cultures. This was called the *Hellenistic* period.

Although Greek democracy survived the fall of Athens, it never fully recovered from the blow. After a long period of decline, it finally disappeared in 30 B.C. with the Roman invasion. The Greek story is long, complex, colorful, fascinating, and dramatic, with the various city states vying with each other. There were several attempts to improve their democratic system, but the times were not right. However, the Greeks contributed an enormous amount in all areas of human thought and activity, not only in politics, commerce, and colonizing, but in philosophy, science, architecture, and the arts, and thereby to The Human Experiment.

Chapter 7
A New European Beginning

The *Renaissance,* which in the French language means "re-birth," is the term used to describe the activity, spirit, or time of the great revival of art, literature, and learning in Europe beginning in the 1300's and extending into the 1600's. During this time artists and scholars began to support the idea of individual freedom, and the idea became a cultural force that spread throughout most of northern Europe and brought about the transition from the Middle Ages to the modern world.

The transition actually began during the Middle Ages as Christian philosophers kept trying to bring together the ideas of the Greek philosophers, and the doctrines of Christianity. The Christian theory of the nature of the Universe followed the tradition begun by Plato; it held that ideas are the real things in the Universe, that they exist apart from objects, in some way determine the form the objects will take, and that the ideas for the objects exist in God's mind. For example, the tree which we see is not "real," as it can exist only because of the idea of it; therefore it is the *idea* of the tree which is the real thing. Thus, he real things of the Universe are not the individual objects of our experience, but the ideas which determine them.

Thus the Christians taught that ideas for things existed in the mind of God, that they molded matter into the things in the Universe, and that the idea could exist without matter.

However, toward the end of the Middle Ages some philosophers took an opposite view. They decided to stop trying to cram Nature into the later Greek theories of ideas, and instead returned to the original approach of the first Greek philosophers which was to study Nature directly. Their theory of the nature of the Universe was that the real things in the Universe are the individual objects which we experience, and that ideas of them are thoughts created in our own minds.

The first tradition had been that in which religion had flourished; out of the second tradition came the Renaissance and the development of science (unknowingly a return to the first humans' studies of cause and effect in the workings of the Natural Environment.)

During this second tradition, revolutionary discoveries were made. In 1543 Nicolaus Copernicus theorized that Earth and the other planets revolve around the sun, rather than the opposite as had previously been thought. Because this conflicted with a passage in the Bible, for his personal safety he had the publication of his work withheld until after his death. In 1609 Johannes Kepler discovered that planets follow elliptical and not circular orbits, which led to other important discoveries. Galileo Galilei stated that theories were valid only if they could be proved by practical experiment. He was the first to use a telescope to observe the skies, made important discoveries in astronomy, and verified Copernicus. He thought the Church would welcome his discoveries about the nature of the Universe, but in 1633 he was brought before the Inquisition in Rome and was made to renounce all his beliefs and writings supporting the Copernican theory.

As we have seen, this system of censorship to control the people began much earlier (as seen in Chapter 3), and was revved in Sumer (as seen in Chapter 5) and now it was again revived. Again the individual person was stopped from moving toward the human goal, because the power-seeking persons in the Establishment liked and depended upon the way things were, and did not want change. Consequently they consciously and purposely tried to suppress new ideas, and tried to kill the progressive, balanced thinking system (HLS) dedicated to the advancement of human thought and knowledge through a partnership of logical and magical thinking, because they wanted magical thinking to dominate so that they could keep their power.

But the spirit of the Renaissance prevailed. Many world masterpieces of architecture, literature, painting, and sculpture were created by persons such as Cervantes, Hans Holbein, Leonardo da Vinci, Raphael, and William Shakespeare. Renaissance scholars, including Desiderius Erasmus and Saint Thomas More, developed a humanist philosophy, which stressed the importance of persons and their enjoyment of life and influenced many political and social movements of modern times.

The humanist philosophy also inspired the *Reformation*, a strong religious movement in the 1500's for reforming the Roman Catholic Church, which led to the establishment of Protestant churches in Germany, England, and many other countries. For many reasons discontent with the Church had been building for some time, and it finally exploded on the issue of "indulgence, " which in the Roman Catholic Church is the pardon of temporal punishment due for "sin." Until the sale of Indulgences was made unlawful by the Council of Trent in 1562, their sale was commonplace, and it was this abuse which Martin Luther first denounced. Under the protection of a German prince, on October 31, 1517 Luther posted on the Church door at Wittenberg 95 propositions for consideration. Luther had not intended a break with Rome, but open attack on the doctrines and authority of the Church followed and led to Luther's breach with the Church in 1520. The Reformation ultimately led to freedom of dissent.

Wood-block printing had been invented by the Chinese around 770, and around 1440 movable type was invented, which resulted in the invention of the printing press, and in a quantum jump in printing and the spread of information, education, and knowledge.

Exploration and commerce expanded rapidly. The spirit of the times called for enjoyment of the pleasurable things in life: tasty foods, elegant clothes, and elaborate homes. Merchants were encouraged to bring fine goods of all kinds from distant lands to European markets. To meet the demands of the merchants, adventurous sailors opened new sea routes to the Far East to avoid the difficult land routes across the Middle East and Asia. Other sea routes led to the Americas after Christopher Columbus made his first voyage there in 1492.

As goods poured into Europe from distant lands a commercial revolution developed. Gold and silver imports created a new kind of wealth. Investment opportunities were provided by the creation of joint-stock companies. These raised money to do business by selling shares of stock to a number of individuals, and formed the basis of the corporations of today. Also, the first stock exchanges were established.

European standards of living rose with the growth of commerce and the use of goods from other regions. European markets were supplied with luxurious chintz fabrics, porcelains, rugs, and silks. Foods from distant lands included bananas, cocoa, coffee, lemons, oranges, and tea. However, in the same period a slave trade developed with Africa.

The expansion of overseas commerce led to the establishment of European colonies in many countries. Some of these, chiefly in tropical countries, were established almost entirely as trading centers. Some served as temporary outposts where European manufactured goods were exchanged for raw materials, but many other colonies became permanent. They included the English colony of Virginia, the French colony of Quebec, and the Spanish colonies of Mexico and Peru.

As the great period called the Renaissance came to a close, there began during the 1600's and 1700's a new great period, an intellectual revolution which swept over Europe called the *Age of Reason* (also called the *Enlightenment*). Traditional principles that had served scholars for hundreds of years were discarded. The leading thinkers of the era insisted that reason was the sole test of truth.

In the 16th Century the philosopher Francis Bacon completely separated religion and philosophy, saying that the doctrines of religion could not be proved by thinking, and that by studying the likenesses and differences among things, one could discover the laws of objects in the Universe and come to an understanding of it.

The most important contribution of the Age of Reason was probably the development of the modern scientific method, very briefly described: a method of research in which a problem is identified, relevant data are gathered, a hypothesis is formulated, and the hypothesis is empirically tested. The hypothesis is not accepted as valid until every effort to disprove it has failed. Using this method scientists applied the reasoning process to their studies of basic natural laws, and organized general rules for reaching scientific conclusions that are still followed today.

(The classic example of the spirit of the scientific method is a story Richard Dawkins tells about what he calls "a formative influence on my undergraduate self." It was "the response of a respected elder statesman of the Oxford Zoology Department when a visiting lecturer publicly disproved his favorite theory. The old man strode to the front of the lecture hall, shook the lecturer warmly by the hand, and declared in ringing emotional tones: 'My dear fellow, I wish to thank you. I have been wrong these fifteen years.' And we clapped our hands red.")

(I see this as an example also of the Human Learning System...HLS... when it is successfully in action.)

One of the steps of the scientific method is careful experimentation. To carry out such experimentation scientists needed precise instruments, and their needs were met by inventors of the era. Galileo had already invented the telescope, and now many important new instruments were developed including the microscope, sextant, slide rule, chronometer, air pump, and adding machine.

Isaac Newton revolutionized astronomy by devising his theory of gravitation, which explains Kepler's laws of planetary motion, and also explains the motion of the Moon, the Earth, and the tides. Benjamin Franklin and Alessandro Volta discovered the nature of electricity. Robert Boyle, Antoine Lavoisier, and Joseph Priestley founded modern chemistry. Rene Descartes invented analytic geometry, and William Harvey discovered how blood circulates in the human body.

The scientific method was so successful in solving problems of Nature that some philosophers applied its principles to human problems. A group of French scholars used the tests of reason with problems of economics, education, government, and religion. The French scholars, known as the *philosophes*, attacked many evils of the times. These evils included religious intolerance, superstition, tyranny, unjust laws, and the slave trade. The most famous member of the French group probably was Voltaire. Others included Montesquieu, Denis Diderot, and Jean Jacques Rousseau. Their writings not only attacked evils, but also expressed a basic faith that symbolized the spirit of the era: belief in the human ability to solve problems, with reason as the most important tool.

The Age of Reason was also a period of achievement in the arts. The form of the modern novel was developed by Henry Fielding. The poem took on new brilliance in famous couplets written by Alexander Pope. Great painters of the era included Thomas Gainsborough, Francisco Goya, William Hogarth, Rembrandt, Sir Joshua Reynolds, and Antoine

Watteau. Many modern forms of music such as the concerto, opera, symphony, and oratorio were developed. Outstanding composers of the period included Johann Sebastian Bach, George Frederic Handel, Joseph Haydn, Wolfgang Amadeus Mozart, and, somewhat later, Ludwig van Beethoven (1770-1827).

Two powerful political forces, democracy and nationalism, took shape during the 1600's and 1700's. Democracy developed from revolutions that established the right of people to govern themselves and ended despotism (absolute control by a ruler) in England, America, and France.

Nationalism developed from the strong feelings of national pride that united the people of each country as they fought for their democratic ideals.

The English revolution of the 1600's was the first important attack in modern times on the absolute power of kings, and was stimulated by the democratic ideas that had developed during the Age of Reason. A republic called a commonwealth was established in England in 1649, but as a republic England came under the rule of Oliver Cromwell, a Puritan leader, who ruled as a dictator. The monarchy was restored in 1660, but the English people continued to fight for a strong voice in the government. In 1688 James II was deposed during the "Glorious Revolution" and William and Mary took the throne. The English revolutionary movement ended in 1689, during which year parliament adopted the Bill of Rights assuring the basic rights of the English people. It took away most powers of the English monarch, guaranteed the liberty of the English people, and provided legal grounds for people to revolt against a bad government. This idea spread to many other countries, chiefly through the works of John Locke, a political scholar who was probably the most influential political writer of the period.

The American revolution was based chiefly on the right of people to revolt, which had been established during the English revolution. The American colonists restated it in the Declaration of Independence of July 4, 1776, which was written by a committee headed by Thomas Jefferson. The committee borrowed from the works of Locke and other political writers, but the language of the Declaration had a special force.

Such phrases as "all men are created equal" made it one of the most important documents in the history of human liberty.

After a long, bloody, revolutionary war (1775-1783) British rule in the American colonies was ended, and a new nation, the United States of America, was formed. The first system of government, established by the Articles of Confederation, proved unsatisfactory, so a new system of government was set up in 1789. Its Constitution established the United States as a republic (a state in which the supreme power rests in the body of citizens entitled to vote and is exercised by representatives chosen directly or indirectly by them) and framed a system of federalism that divided power between national and state governments. In 1791 the first 10 amendments to the constitution came into force. (Chapter 9 tells how a crucial 11th Amendment was proposed by Jefferson and Madison, but very unfortunately was rejected by the Congress.) Known as the Bill of Rights, the ten state the basic rights of all citizens. The United States Constitution became a model for the constitutions of many other countries, including most of the Latin-American republics.

During the American revolution and the early years of the republic strong feelings of democracy developed in the United States, and since then democracy has become the chief rallying point of American nationalism. (We will continue to consider the development of the United States of America in Chapter 9.)

The French revolution (1789-1799) was a great political and social upheaval, marked by disorder and violence. During the First French Republic (1792-1799) most symbols of despotism or privilege in France were wiped out. Titles of nobility were eliminated and "citizen" became the only French title. The French revolutionists issued a great document of democratic principles: the Declaration of the Rights of Man.

The French revolutionary struggle was climaxed by a reign of terror under the rule of radical leaders such as Danton and Robespierre. The guillotine, a beheading device, became a symbol of the French revolution, and thousands of aristocrats and many citizens who opposed the radicals were guillotined. During this period the French armies won many victories against foreign enemies of revolutionary France. In 1794 the period of terror ended, and soon afterward the nation came under the stern rule of Napoleon Bonaparte. A brilliant military tactician, he led France to victory after victory until in 1812 the French controlled most of Western Europe. The French soldiers fought hard to defend and spread the democratic principles in which they believed, and their battle cry of "liberty, equality, fraternity" stirred the democratic and nationalistic feelings of many peoples. Almost all the European monarchs lost most of their powers in revolutionary movements that swept over much of Europe.

Ironically, Napoleon made himself Emperor in 1804; but he was defeated in the Battle of Waterloo in 1815, and during the Congress of Vienna the great powers (aka The Establishment) tried by restoring monarchies to smother the democratic and nationalistic forces that were sweeping over Europe. Most of their efforts failed, and democratic movements succeeded in many countries, notably in France where in 1875 a lasting republican government was established. By the 1880's many nations of Western Europe had constitutions and some had democratic institutions. At the same time strongly nationalistic people had unified many small states and formed new nations, such as Austria-Hungary, Germany, and Italy.

Through colonial wars of independence in Latin America, by 1824 most of the countries had been freed from European rule. New, independent nations included Argentina, Bolivia, Brazil, Chile, Columbia, Ecuador, Peru, and Venezuela.

Chapter 8
Industrialism

During the late 1700's and the 1800's an industrial revolution changed most of the Western World. Machines replaced many hand tools that people had used for thousands of years, and with the inventions of new machines and steam engines (1769) to run them, vast quantities of goods could be produced rapidly. Never before had humans been able to make such enormous use of Earth's natural resources, and this industrialism changed the lives of millions of people (and began the over-consumption of our natural resources, and the over-populating of our planet). When the era began, most families lived in farm areas, and the towns and villages served chiefly as market centers for the farmers. As industry developed, factories were built in many towns, and these towns grew rapidly into industrial cities. People streamed into the cities to take jobs tending the machines in the factories. Railroads and waterways were built to link many cities, and also provided transportation between the cities and the farmlands, forests, and mines. The invention of the telegraph furnished instant communication between distant places.

The growth of industrialism brought social changes of great importance. A middle class appeared, and its members were neither nobles nor peasants; most of them were businessmen and wealthy landowners, and this new middle class grew in size and influence. Its members owned most of the factories, hired the workers, and operated the banks, mines, railroads, and shops. Most members of the middle class believed that business should be regulated by supply and demand without government controls. This idea formed the basis of the economic system known as *capitalism,* and its theoretical principles were set forth by the Scottish economist Adam Smith.

Unfortunately, the rapid growth of industrialism produced many problems, especially that most factory workers, including small children, were poorly paid and suffered great hardships. Also, it was not permitted to form labor unions, and working conditions were not regulated by law. The situation led to widespread attacks against the evils of the capitalist system, and *socialism* became the chief rallying point for many persons who opposed the capitalist system. The Socialists wanted to put all industrial production under the control of governments through non-violent, democratic process. However, Karl Marx, a German writer and social philosopher, believed that the change could be made only through revolutionary socialism, and to distinguish it from evolutionary socialism, in 1848 he and Friedrich Engels, another German writer and social philosopher, wrote and published the "Communist Manifesto." It called for the workers of the world to unite and to revolt against the middle class and set up state-owned economic systems. Their slogan was: "Workers of the world unite; you have nothing to lose but your chains."

Many reforms supported by members of various social movements were adopted generally during the 1800's, and in several countries workers won the right to form labor unions. Laws regulating working conditions in factories were passed in Great Britain and the United States during the 1830's, and later many other countries also passed laws that improved the conditions of industrial workers. Great Britain and Germany pioneered in social legislation that provided accident, sickness, and unemployment insurance for industrial employees. By the late 1800's most industrial nations had laws that regulated working conditions and also raised the people's standards of living.

The industrial nations needed large supplies of raw materials for their factories, and the vast continents of Africa and Asia had these materials in abundance. Africa and Asia also had millions of people who still used ancient tools of production. These two continents provided good markets for the wide variety of manufactured goods being produced in the industrial nations of Europe. Consequently the European nations established many colonies in Africa and Asia during the 1800's to insure a flow of raw materials and to control large markets. European colonial rule extended over most of Africa, and Great Britain and France were the leading colonial powers there. Nearly a third of Asia came under the colonial rule of Great Britain, France, The Netherlands, Portugal, and Spain. China had closed most of its ports to Europeans but they were re-opened in 1842 after Britain defeated China in the Opium War.

By the late 1800's huge European empires had spread over most of the world. The largest empires were those of Great Britain, France, and Germany, and important colonies were also established by Belgium, The Netherlands, and Portugal. This colonial expansion became known as *imperialism*. In 1823 the United States acted to protect the independent countries of Latin America from European colonial expansion through the *Monroe Doctrine*. However, the influence of the United States over Latin America was often called imperialism too.

Industrialism and imperialism created an era called "Europe's Wonderful Century" by some persons, who happened to be born in the upper or middle class, but not called that by those who happened to be born in one of the filthy, wretched, dangerous slum districts of a city. Most European nations had become economically wealthy and militarily strong, and ruled vast regions of the world through powerful colonial systems, but personal wealth was far from spread equitably, and poverty and ill health were rampant among the lower class.

At the same time the arts, scholarship, and sciences reached high levels of development. In England in 1830 the geologist Charles Lyell published his *Principles of Geology* in which he recognized that the Earth has been shaped gradually over geological time by the same slow forces operating today, i.e. surface erosion and internal forces that cause volcanoes and earthquakes. As the ages pass, sections of land are uplifted and eroded, revealing the fossilized remains of life forms that existed many thousands of years ago. Building on Lyell's work, in 1859 English naturalist Charles Darwin published *On the Origin of Species*. Prior to the discoveries of Lyell and Darwin nearly everyone in the Western world believed that the Earth and all its inhabitants had been created just a few thousand years ago. They thought the geography of the Earth and the character of the individual species in it had not changed significantly since the beginning of the Universe. Fossilized extinct species such as dinosaurs were "explained" as being the races of giants alluded to in the Bible.

Lyell and Darwin shattered this static, contained worldview with their vision of an ancient, dynamic Earth on which species have constantly been emerging and becoming extinct. Darwin and Alfred Wallace, independently but concurrently, recognized that all present species are derived from earlier species by the process of natural selection; thus all species on Earth are related by descent from common ancestors. Sigmund Freud (1856-1939), an Austrian neurologist, founded psychoanalysis, and described the unconscious mind.

The European way of life during the1800's formed the most advanced "civilization" the world had ever known, and the United States, Canada, and some other countries of the Western Hemisphere were rapidly developing along the European pattern. In contrast, most nations of Africa and Asia remained at "primitive" levels. The arrogance of the European nations met with little challenge, and as a result certain attitudes shaped the basic philosophy of the era, notably the belief that it was right for millions of colonial peoples to be ruled by European nations, and that capitalism, although subject to reforms, would develop as the only important economic system.

However, the first half of the 1900's was a period of great change, perhaps the most rapid and widespread changes in human history, and by the 1960's the huge European empires had collapsed, most of the attitudes of the previous era were shattered, the costliest and most destructive wars in history were fought, and political and social upheavals had overturned many long-established governments, the first one being that of Russia, for the following reasons.

By the late 1800's most industrial nations had laws that regulated working conditions and also raised the people's standards of living. However, wealthy people had grown more wealthy and had gained in governmental power, while the working people had become more poor and out of governmental power. Consequently Democratic Socialists continued to try to gain power in government through elections, and the Marxists continued to call for a class war that would cross national boundaries and through violence would overthrow capitalism, which all kinds of Socialists believed to be an unworkable, unfair, inhuman, and self-destructive system.

Marx had thought that the revolution would begin in a highly-industrialized European nation, probably England, but through a quirk it began in one of the least-industrialized European nations: Russia. This occurred because Russia and its allies were fighting Germany in WW I, which had begun in 1914, and in 1917 the Russian army began to retreat. Consequently the Marxist international revolutionaries adapted quickly and seized the moment by persuading the retreating Russian soldiers and starving masses of civilians to free themselves from the cruel, repressive Czarist regime and build a new government ruled by the people. The Czarist regime was overthrown but, unfortunately, the new government became a repressive dictatorship which was neither socialist, nor communist, and should not have been given either name.

World War I was fought mostly in Europe but it involved most of the world's great powers. In November of 1918, after four years of terrible fighting and misery, a stalemate occurred, and an Armistice was reached, ending a war in which 65 million men had served in the armies, an estimated 10 million persons had been killed and double that number wounded. Four great empires had disappeared: Germany, Austria-Hungary, Turkey, and Russia. Under the Treaty of Versailles the Allies imposed unrealistic penalties on Germany and divided much of the world in irrational, unworkable ways. In 1920 the international organization called the League of Nations was created to prevent another war, but the large member nations had no intention of carrying out the ideas of the League, plus which the US refused to join in spite of the fact that its President Wilson was one of its most ardent founders and supporters. As a result of the irrational Treaty of Versailles, a world-wide economic depression, and other factors, there arose totalitarian, militaristic regimes in Italy, Germany, Spain, and Japan. In spite of the League, in 1935 the Italian fascist dictator Mussolini invaded Ethiopia, a small, ancient, undefended country in east central Africa, sending his air fleet to bomb cities, towns, and villages indiscriminately and killing or wounding thousands of peace-loving persons.

World War II actually began in 1936. The Spanish fascist General Francisco Franco had been exiled to the Canary Islands, but he escaped to Spanish Morocco and funded by foreign fascist money he formed an army and invaded the duly-elected Republic of Spain. The Spanish men, women, and children fought like tigers to defend their country, and would have defeated the invader had not Mussolini poured in Italian troops, and Hitler, the Nazi dictator, poured in German troops and equipment, including tanks and war planes and pilots, which machine gunned, blasted, and bombed the poorly equipped Spaniards. After three years of bloody fighting and destruction the loyal citizens were defeated, Franco became the fascist dictator of Spain, and an era of vengeful murder and suppression began.

Then on September 1,1939 the Second World War began officially when Hitler ordered his Nazi troops to invade Poland, and then France, whereupon Britain immediately declared war on Germany and sent troops to help defend France. However they were hopelessly outnumbered and out gunned and forced onto the beach at Dunkerque, on the French side of the English Channel. Almost every English boat afloat, civilian and Navy, made many trips to transport the soldiers to England, in spite of being under heavy German fire by air and land. German bombers set the city of London afire in preparation for an assault across the Channel, but the RAF shot down enough German planes to prevent the crossing.

On June 22, 1941, Germany invaded the Soviet Union, bringing that nation, under Premier Joseph Stalin, into the war. On December 7, 1941 Japan attacked Pearl Harbor, bringing the US, under President Franklin D. Roosevelt, into the war. There followed terrible fighting everywhere, on land, sea, and in the air until finally, on May 7, 1945, after Hitler's suicide Germany surrendered unconditionally. Italy had already surrendered, and in August, 1945, while US troops were preparing to invade Japan's home islands, US President Harry S. Truman ordered the dropping of the atomic bomb on Hiroshima. Then, as the Japanese still would not surrender, an atomic bomb was dropped on Nagasaki, causing Japan to surrender on August 14, 1945, thereby bringing to an end the costliest and most destructive war in human history.

To help bring peace, cooperation, and prosperity to the people of Earth, in 1945 the United Nations Organization (UN) was created, but in1950 North Korea invaded South Korea; in 1957 North Vietnam invaded South Vietnam; and in 1980 war broke out between Iraq and Iran. Then Iraq invaded Kuwait; the US invaded Afghanistan; the US invaded and occupied Iraq; a civil war broke out in Iraq; and in 2009 the US and its allies were still fighting in Iraq and in Afghanistan, all of which seems insane.

During this time science had made great advances. By the 1960's the people of an industrialized country hardly realized how much life had changed. They took for granted atomic energy, automation, radio, color television, refrigerators, color motion pictures, telephones, synthetic materials, and superhighways crowded with automobiles. None of these things had even existed in 1900.

In the 1960's people were also accustomed to great achievements from medical science. In 1900 life expectancy in the United States was 47.3 years, and by the mid 1960's it was 70 years. Also, revolutionary technological inventions altered basic ways of life and thrust humans into the Space Age.

Chapter 9
The Rise of Corporations in the US

To follow the rise of corporations in the United States we need to begin by going back to the time when shiploads of persons went from England to the North American east coast, settled there, and after many struggles prospered. Then a problem arose. The King of England had claimed ownership of the land and had given the corporation named the British East India Company the power to rule. To recognize the extent of this power we need to consider a brief history of corporations.

As noted, probably the first business corporations were created in the Sumerian cities when groups of citizens bought and sold land as corporations and as syndicates. Modern day business corporations were conceived over 600 years ago when governments began granting charters allowing the formation of corporations by persons which made it legal for them to operate in nations other than their own. Within a nation whose government granted a charter, people were still required to obey laws against murder, theft, etc., and there still tended to be some efforts to respect and to help others. But the corporate charters gave persons permission to do anything in certain places outside the home nation, including thieving and murdering, which would bring it goods or money. Following are some of the more famous English charters:

- In 1407 King Henry the Fourth of England chartered the "Company of Merchants and Adventurers," (ancestor of the East India Company) granting it exclusive rights to send cloth to market between the mouth of the Somme River (in northeast France) and the tip of Denmark.
- In 1553 the Crown chartered the Muscovy Company, granting it monopoly privilege over certain trade routes to Russia.
- In 1553 the Africa Company was chartered, granting it special privileges to pursue the slave trade.

- In 1557 the Spanish Company was chartered, granting it special privileges and monopolies to control the wine and olive oil trade with Spain and Portugal.
- In 1578 the Eastlund Company was chartered, granting it sole privilege to carry on trade with Scandinavian countries, Poland, and the east coast of the Baltic, and was also granted additional authority to make laws, impose fines, and imprison people.
- In 1581 the Levant Company was chartered, giving it special privileges to trade with Turkey.
- In 1592 it merged with the Turkey Company and the Venice Company (in which Queen Elizabeth was a shareholder) to form the East India Company.
- In 1600 the East India Company was given a charter in perpetuity and given exclusive rights to trade in specified areas of Europe, East and West Asia, and North and West Africa. It acquired unequaled trade privileges from the Mogul emperors in India, and began to reap large profits by exporting textiles and tea. As Mogul power declined, the company intervened in Indian political affairs. Its agent, Robert Clive, defeated the rival French East India Company (1751-60, and Warren Hastings, the first governor general of British India, assumed more control of the company. After the Indian Mutiny of 1857 Britain took over India's administration and the company was dissolved.

The mission of these and other global corporations was to buy cheap, sell dear, limit or prevent competition, vacuum out resources, display fierce violence, perpetuate violence to people, species, and places, destroy existing cultures and social relationships, replace independence with dependence, eradicate people's sense of their own histories, get people to internalize the corporation's values, myths, and worldviews, create a class of bureaucrats and civil servants to serve their needs, define people as subjects, objects, property, and invisible, control all dispute resolution, raise armies, navies, and wage war, write laws and doctrines which legalized and institutionalized the corporation's destructive and dominating acts, enforce laws and impose punishments including executions. In other words, to govern dictatorially. Although the term "fascist" had not yet come into use it is clear that it applied to these corporations.

Thus the renegade corporations became the instruments for the nations to colonize. As corporations succeeded in their dictatorial attitudes and ways abroad, they promoted dictatorial attitudes and ways at home, so even there the rich became richer and more powerful, and the poor became poorer and more powerless.

During the late 1500's when persons left England in large numbers to colonize the Americas, much of the transportation was provided at a profitable price by the East India Company. It had claimed parts of North America, and had deeded land to the Virginia Company, which was the name of two English colonization companies created by King James in 1606. One founded the Plymouth Company, and the other, known as the London Company, founded colonies in the south, notably the settlement of Jamestown in 1606 on Chesapeake Bay. The company-owned Commonwealth of Virginia extended from the Atlantic Ocean to the Mississippi River.

In 1620, seeking religious freedom the Pilgrims arrived in America on the *Mayflower,* a ship chartered from the East India Company, which had made three previous trips with colonists.

Through the 1600s and early 1700s the Company largely took control of north America and forced unfair trading restrictions on American small businessmen, including taxes on commodities, and interfered in colonial life and government. The people appealed to the King for justice, but to no avail. Consequently on July 4, 1776 the thirteen American Colonies proclaimed a Declaration of Independence and fought a long, hard war for freedom. At the cost of the deaths of many brave persons they won the war and instituted democracy in the New World by creating and implementing the Constitution of the democratic Republic of the United States of America.

During the writing of the Constitution Thomas Jefferson and James Madison, two of the new nation's greatest statesmen, were well aware of the danger of powerful corporations, because they knew that the American Revolution was in substantial degree a revolt against the tyrannical domination of colonial economic and political life by the greatest multinational corporation of its age: the above noted British

East India Company. (It owned the tea which Sam Adams and friends dumped overboard into Boston Harbor.) Therefore Jefferson and Madison worked diligently to have an 11th Amendment included in the original Constitution to join the other ten amendments which together are known as the Bill of Rights.

The proposed Amendment would have prohibited "monopolies in commerce," which would have made it illegal for corporations to own other corporations, or to give money to politicians or to otherwise influence elections. Corporations would be chartered by the states for the primary purpose of "serving the public good." They would not possess the legal status of natural persons but of "artificial persons." They would have only those legal attributes which the law saw fit to give them. They could not possess the same bundle of rights which actual flesh and blood persons enjoy. Neither the subsequent 14th Amendment of the US Constitution, nor any provision of that document would protect the artificial entities known as corporations. Although Jefferson and Madison continued to fight hard for the amendment, in the end it was not adopted because a majority of persons in the first Congress believed that already existing state laws governing corporations were adequate for constraining corporate power. What followed shows that they were very wrong.

After the ratification of the Constitution by the States, some persons thought our country needed heavy industry in order to make its place in the modern world. Large amounts of funding were needed and to raise them the federal government and the states' governments issued charters for private persons to form corporations which would be considered artificial persons, with the understanding that they would be monitored closely and prevented from doing anything that went against the public good. This surveillance was necessary because in a capitalist system a corporation, having no brain, mind, or conscience, is a robot programed to make as much money as possible in the shortest time for its officers and investors, regardless of the effect on anyone else.

For 100 years after the US Constitution was ratified, state and federal officials watched the activities of corporations closely and revoked their charters immediately if they went against the public good in any way.

However, during that time railroads were continuously expanded, in the east and westward, and the railroad corporations became increasingly rich and powerful. Consequently their attorneys kept bringing cases into courts to get them to say that corporations were real persons and entitled to those rights. President Abraham Lincoln recognized what the corporate attorneys were seeking and consequently he wrote: "I see in the near future a crisis approaching that unnerves me and causes me to tremble for the safety of my country.... Corporations have been enthroned and an era of corruption in high places will follow, and the money power of the country will endeavor to prolong its reign by working upon the prejudices of people until all wealth is aggregated in a few hands and the Republic is destroyed."

Unfortunately his dire prediction has almost come true, beginning with a criminal act by an attorney, formerly a railroad corporation's president, who took the matter into his own hands. Acting as a court reporter, in 1886 he wrote a false summary of a court's action (called a "headnote") involving Santa Clara County and the Southern Pacific Railroad Corporation in which he said the court had given the corporation the Constitutional rights of a real person. The court's official record shows that this was a false statement, but using this criminal loophole corporations quickly began to do things very much not serving the public good.

The results for us Americans are that several of our corporations, along with those of other nations, have become global, have grown to enormous size, and being robots with no brain, mind, conscience, or morality, are being used by their officers to become the modern day agents of the Dark Culture, over-consuming or destroying our life-sustaining natural resources, and systematically destroying our Constitution and our democratic way of life as fast as they can in order to increase their corporative powers and profits.

It comes close to committing "the perfect crime:" the corporative structure is a robot programmed to follow the rules of the accepted capitalistic "free market" system, so the CEO's feel that they are innocent of any wrong-doing, and so do the stockholders. Members of Congress do nothing to stop this crime, because they receive large amounts of corporative money to use for their reelection, and eventually for them to become lobbyists for the corporations.

Some examples of corporative crimes, among many others, are that they have used the huge corporative fortunes to: take over and genetically alter the world's food supply; drive small and medium sized farms out of business; buy and corrupt our national media; rig our elective process in the year 2000 to make two of their kind president and vice president so as to further their schemes; hire thousands of corporate representatives called "lobbyists" to influence our government to buy their products and to use them to make war so that they could extend their spheres of global influence and increase their powers and fortunes; and, assisted by their servants, those radio and television commentators and newspaper writers who twist information and promote fear and hatred, have created an atmosphere of fear and hatred which, under the guise of fighting "terrorism," has resulted in a step by step process of taking away from us the rights guaranteed to us by our Constitution. Hence the almost incomprehensibly, terrible fact is that our government, and consequently our personal lives, are being run by the agents of a *robot.* By telling gross lies these agents have made it into a horrible, murdering monster, using its power and money to cause the waging of oil-and-empire-seeking wars which have killed many thousands of innocent civilians and several thousands of our American soldiers, and wounded or maimed many more thousands of civilians and soldiers, all completely unnecessarily.

This insanity began during the presidency of George *H. W.* Bush. A group of power-hungry persons called "neocons" decided that it was time for the United states to dominate the rest of the world, and devised a plan to achieve this with military force. Eventually it came to be called "The Project for the New American Century," PNAC, and it became part of the policy of the George *W.* Bush administration after his so-called "election" in the year 2000.

The plan was to create an American Empire by invading the Middle East and taking over the supplies and production of oil. They were hoping for an excuse to put the plan into action, and they got it on September 11, 2001 when after four large US passenger airplanes were hijacked, two were flown into the two towers of the World Trade Center in New York

City, destroying them and killing 3,000 persons, another was flown into the Pentagon, and another intended to be flown into the White House was caused to crash in a field in Pennsylvania when its passengers attacked the hijackers.

The Bush administration blamed Afghanistan and attacked it. Then they lied and said that Iraq had "weapons of mass destruction" and attacked it with bombs and missiles, killing thousands of civilians. Before the two attacks Bush and his Administration were told by everyone with knowledge and experience (including his father, George H.W. Bush) that they could not possibly succeed in occupying Iraq, and would cause horrible consequences for the US and everyone else involved, and that is exactly what has occurred, except for the Global Corporations, who have made billions of dollars in profits, mostly illegally.

The Bush Administration's policies have torn our social fabric to pieces, cost the US taxpayers billions of dollars, put the Nation trillions of dollars in debt, and the fighting continues. The war in Iraq (in 2008) has become a full-scale civil war, and Bush is sending in 20 thousand more American soldiers to try to quell it in order to be able to stay in Iraq so that our corporations can have Iraq's oil... and he does nothing to promote alternative energy.

In addition, in the 2004 election the President and Vice President and their team purposefully brought religious groups into the election process in order to, as Lincoln wrote, "prolong their reign by working upon the prejudices of people." The duty of the President and Vice President is to bring the people together; instead, they managed to "divide and rule" and bring chaos.

All this horror brings us to the subject of "fascism." In defining it the American Heritage Illustrated Encyclopedic Dictionary of 1987 describes exactly what has come into being here: *"fascism* - A philosophy or system of government that advocates or exercises a dictatorship of the extreme right, typically through the merging of state and business leadership, together with an ideology of belligerent nationalism." Today we can see that this is exactly what occurred in the nations which started WW II, and that after that terrible war to kill fascism, it has risen in one of the "victor" nations, the US itself (Note: That was the last time this definition was included in an American Heritage Dictionary. Now they refer only to Mussolini, Hitler, etc., not to anything which could be identified with the U.S.A.)

This merging of state and business leadership, together with its ideology of belligerent nationalism, has occurred in the U.S. under the leadership of the ever-growing size and power of the giant corporations. This is a terrible tragedy for several reasons, especially because the people of the U.S. could be the ones to lead the way to world peace and the completion of the fourth human paradise on Earth. However, fascism is always there in the wings, waiting to dash on stage at the first opportunity, and it is militantly anti-democracy.

Fascists say that democracy is too slow, too cumbersome, too inefficient to get the things done which need to be done. The question to ask fascists is, "What things do you think need to be done?" We have witnessed their response in their actions which led to WW II. Fascists think that they are the state, that the people exist to serve the State, and that the first things to be done when they gain control of a nation are to establish a secret police system, spy on everyone, institute torture, murder suspected dissenters or throw them into prisons, put everyone else into uniform, and begin attacking other nations to steal their natural resources.

What the fascists do not understand is that becoming and being human was an invention of the individual person. Therefore they also do not understand what this means, which is that the entire human system, the culture, must be built around the needs of the individual person during his/her entire lifetime. It must help persons to develop their potential to become and be human. This is the *purpose* of the human system. If it does not fulfill its purpose, it has no valid reason to exist.

Fortunately, during the midterm elections in November of 2006 the people of the U.S. voted for and elected senators and representatives who said they were against the wars, and enough of these persons were elected to gain control of both houses of Congress. In addition, the polls show that the vast majority of Americans do not like Bush, hate what he has done, and want the new Congress to stop his plans and get us out of Iraq, and that the vast majority of Iraqis also want us to get out. It had been hoped by the voters that the persons they elected would not back down on their promises to the voters to find a way to end the war diplomatically and to bring the troops home. Very unfortunately, the new Congress has not been able to change the basic system and so bowed down to Bush, even though he has been caught lying to us and breaking the laws in our Constitution, and the people are totally disappointed, disgusted, and angry. It is clear that Bush & Company want to keep his wars going, and even start new ones if they can.

It is now May of 2008, and something very surprising and wonderful has been occurring: a white woman and a black man, both US senators, are campaigning to be the Democratic candidate for president in this year's election. They each appear to have sufficient intelligence, education, courage, and sense of honor and loyalty to lead us as we desperately need to be led.

For several years there has been a public effort to impeach Bush and/or Cheney, but the Congress apparently would not even consider it. Perhaps they were not aware that the impeachment process is not intended to accuse or indict someone, but to consider the reasons put forward for the impeachment. During the process the record of the person being considered may enable the person to explain it in a satisfactory way, or apologize, or resign, or whatever.

It is now July of 2008. After a long and hotly contested and very close primary session the black man has won the Democratic candidacy to be President. The former (woman) candidate is working hard to help his campaign, the polls show him leading over the Republic candidate, and the movement to impeach Bush is gathering momentum. Impeachment is crucially important to the future stability of our nation, because Bush has been continuously breaking the laws (i.e. in our Constitution) which are supposed to maintain the balance of power, and he has been getting away with it, and unless he is legally stopped now this will set a destructive precedent for future presidents. It is amazing that Congress has not acted. Very fortunately, recently a U.S. Representative in Congress (Dem. Dennis Kucinich) has read into the Congressional Record, Articles of Impeachment against Bush, which means that the Judiciary Committee must take action.

The Republican candidate for President is desperate to win the general election in November, and trying to find any way he can to make the Democratic candidate look incompetent, but the Democratic candidate continues to lead in the polls and hopefully will win the election and that so will other Democratic candidates for offices.

It seems that this could occur, because the people are waking up to the reality of our situation and want to correct it. But nothing is yet certain.

It is now September of 2008, and it looks like it has become a very close race for the presidency. It is now November of 2008 and Barrack Obama, the black candidate, has won!!!!

It seems that the people are beginning to wake up. We have elected a President who represents our country by his ideals and by his being a mixture of our ethnicities, who is intelligent, courageous, and will lead us in working for peace, democracy, and prosperity in the U.S. and in the world. He understands that to succeed we need to build a new culture, and he is working to achieve this.

It is now December 7,2009, Pearl Harbor Day. Unfortunately, instead of bringing our soldiers home, the President is planning to send thousands more soldiers to Afghanistan. This makes no sense at all. Having our troops there only helps our enemies and creates more of them. To bring our troops home would strengthen our nation at home, and raise our prestige abroad.

Fortunately President Obama is taking steps to restore our economy and to create a Universal Health Plan. But we in the U.S. have a fundamental problem which blocks most progress. One way to present our problem is to make a comparison:

> The famous philosopher, Jean Jacques Rousseau, stated that "government is a necessary evil." Obviously necessary, because without it there is chaos. Experience has shown the French people that Rousseau was right, and for that reason they believe in having a government, and of course one that is just. They will tolerate a certain amount of government corruption and ill-behavior, but when the line is crossed they go into the streets and stay there until the situation has been corrected.

Most persons in the U.S. also believe in the necessity of having a government, and that it be just, because without it there would be chaos. However some of the very rich persons, and the business persons who make and keep them and themselves rich, are demonstrating that they do *not* believe in nor desire just government. They want nothing to stand in the way of their making more and more money, and do not care at all about the welfare of others.

Perhaps this is a trend which began because America was seen as the new "land of opportunity," where one should be allowed to make as much money as they could. "Go West young man," and take whatever you desire.

For whatever reason, today these anti-just government, money-and-power-loving persons make up an upper class who give their loyalty to it instead of to their country, and who actually run our government by using their ill-gotten money to bribe politicians, and to own or control the media and use it to propagandize the people.

Chapter 10
Community

A dictionary definition of *community* is: "A group of people living in the same locality and under the same government."

Regarding the *group,* the design of the new community must recognize that the total human group includes each person on planet Earth. Very fortunately we have acquired scientific evidence proving that we really are all one group, one species, one " family." Comparative studies of blood and of genes in persons all over Earth show that we all have the same ancestry, and that the variation among individuals *in* a grouping of persons, is s so much greater than the variations *between* groupings of persons, that the concept of "race" has become meaningless. There is no scientific basis for saying that any one population is genetically superior or inferior to another.

The lack of this knowledge was a main cause of the fall of the first human paradise, and partially a cause of the fall of the second and third ones, and, unless the knowledge is made global, the lack of it may prevent us from building the fourth one. Fortunately, spreading our knowledge that we actually are one family can help us all to work together to create the appropriate *communities* which will comprise and maintain the fourth paradise.

Regarding the *locality*, it has become clear that we humans have taken over the entire surface of our planet and, having interfered with its natural workings, must now all become its stewards. But even though we are one human group, we can not of course all live in one place. We must live in many optimum-sized and optimally-dispersed appropriate communities. Also, we must see that although we are instinctively prone to live in social groups, appropriate human community as we need it to be today requires both physical and mental interaction, and can be created initially only through human mental interaction, i.e. it is a human *idea.* For appropriate community to exist, the idea of it must be created in the minds of living persons, and for it to continue to exist the idea must be maintained in their minds. People can build a cluster of dwellings and call it their community. But if they leave it, the cluster is no longer a community; it is a "ghost town." Indeed our first human ancestors had no dwellings. They created their community in their own minds, carried it with them wherever they went, and wherever they were at a certain moment was their locality.

Because we produce food and have become dependent on doing so, our idea of appropriate community has come to include a physical place, with water and food sources and housing. Therefore we might say that today our idea of appropriate community is a place where individual persons can be born, grow up developing their human potential, produce healthful food and other things ecologically, including housing and transportation facilities, govern themselves democratically, and enjoy life.

Regarding the *government*, a crucial fact revealed by our Story is that the minds of our first human ancestors were guided by the workings of their surrounding natural environment, and that it was within this natural system that persons were motivated and able to create ideas for democratic government, which enormously improved their ability to survive and enjoy life. Therefore our community government must again be guided by the workings of our natural environment.

In regard to children growing up developing their human potential, for information about brain development we turned to the work of researchers of the human brain's evolution, development, and functions. For present purposes the point to be noted is that the children of early humans received the nurturing necessary for their three brains (today four brains) to develop sufficiently for them fo live together cooperatively, and today such an opportunity is far from guaranteed.

However an appropriate human community today will provide that opportunity, because everyone in the community will join in providing it. In "primitive" or "developing" societies parents can still get help from their extended family and other community members, but in "developed" societies today many single mothers or fathers are struggling to make a living and take care of a child or children. Even when there are two parents it is becoming increasingly difficult for them to make a living and meet the needs of their children and themselves. In an appropriate community the care of all children is part of the daily routine of everyone. Also, children need a variety of persons to learn from to meet their developing needs. In fact, experience shows that the "nuclear" family i.e. a father, mother, and child (or children) is a far too dangerous system, which is one reason for the old African saying: "It takes a village to raise a child." In nuclear families the adult(s) has far too much power, along with far too much stress. For a baby to be born or put into anything other than a group community is playing roulette with its life; turn the wheel. and wherever the ball comes to rest selects the home in which it will be raised. Maybe it will be a perfect home, or even an adequate one, but in today's cultural situation the odds are against it.

In a democratic community children learn how to think and act in ways which help them to live healthy and happy lives, and the way children grow up determines what kind of world we will have. Also, even adults need a variety of persons with whom to interact. Sometimes women need to talk to other women, and sometimes men need to talk to other men. This situation provides the best possibility for adult men and women to work out the problems humans can have about relationships, especially sexual ones, in ways which make possible the happiest results for all, including the children.

All things considered, it seems that human community should be built around meeting the physical and mental developmental needs of its children. Not only would it be best for children, but would be best also for adults, thus for all persons, through their life spans.

We can not expect to create ideal communities all over Earth overnight, but we can write and share descriptions of them so as to have a goal to work toward. They will be of all shapes and sizes depending on many factors, such as location, climate, and natural resources. Where possible, each community will grow most of its own food, in private gardens and community gardens which will be ecologically designed.

In addition to the obvious reasons for persons growing food, gardening together is a very enjoyable and enormously successful way of getting to know each other, and feeling the need we have for each other, and for cooperation and the building of friendship and trust, and for transcending what we imagined to be our differences. Adults who grow up in such a community will have developed all four of their brains, and the developed fourth one gives us the wisdom we need today. A wonderful thing that occurs in such a democratic community is the emergence of a *group mind,* which is wiser and more stable than any one mind could be, and is acceptable to everyone because everyone contributes continuously to creating it. (It would be what we have called a "bright culture.")

Community government will be by its own members, all meeting together or through whatever other arrangement they will agree to. The details of the elements will be worked out through planning meetings and experience, and much can be learned from what has already been learned and published by Intentional Communities (ICs). Thanks to the internet today's ICs are linking together, sharing and publishing information, and cooperating with each other in their mutual best interest. (See: The Fellowship for Intentional Communities at ic.org)

On a recent tour my wife and I met a Japanese-American couple who were interned in a prison camp in rugged, open territory during WW II. They are both wonderful persons, born and raised in the US, and as fellow Americans we were ashamed by the terribly unjust way in which they were treated. Nevertheless, when we asked them about it, they had an inspiring story to tell. Their group was dumped into a fenced camp of rude buildings, sparsely furnished, with almost none of their own possessions, and guarded by armed soldiers. The wind blew through cracks in their walls, and they were cold and miserable.

After a while they realized that they were on their own, and that if they were to survive they must organize themselves. They held a meeting, created their own government, and organized themselves into a highly cooperative society, with doctors, nurses, dentists, teachers, and all. Through the war they managed to keep their spirits up, and then to resume their lives; but they never really recovered from the hurt of their unjust treatment by their own country. I asked if there were a book about their internment and they recommended one by Michi Weglyn. I intend to find and read it, because it tells about building a solid community in dire circumstances from the grass roots.

Although we must begin by working through the national governmental institutions we now have, for the long term our human groups and governments must be based on natural criteria, and build from the grass roots up, not from the top down. Perhaps the fourth paradise may be begun by individual persons creating optimum-sized, self-governing, democratic communities in nations, and then linking their communities to each other in their mutual best interest. Eventually they might link their communities with ones in other nations; that would result in nations linking together, sharing information, and cooperating with each other, as has occurred in the European Union. Then communities would begin to organize globally (this is already occurring) and probably there will be a Global Confederation of Communities.

Experience shows us that persons are more likely to fully develop their human potential by being in self-governing, democratic communities, and that this is why our human plan has always been and is to create them. A way to bring our plan sufficiently into our consciousness is to build a model community in each nation, and have a few persons demonstrate how the plan makes possible a viable and desirable way of living. Such communities would be built by skilled and dedicated persons, with the full knowledge and support of the rest of the world. Everyone on Earth would be informed of what was being planned and done, and why.

It is interesting to note that a few years ago everyone on Earth *was* being informed about a model community, not on our planet, but above it. All of the news media of the world were reporting that "Atlantis-Mir" was orbiting Earth with four Russians and six Americans aboard. During space-to-ground interviews each crew member reflected on "the meaning of it all." Typical was, "When we look down at the Earth as space-farers, we don't see borders, we don't see boundaries, we see one Earth where we all came from. We feel that it would be really tremendous if we could all work together toward positive outcomes." (Today we have created also an International Space Station.)

For several reasons it is vitally important that we have already developed an instantaneous, interactive, global communication system, employing satellites, telephone systems, computers, the world-wide web, e-mail, radio, TV, newspapers, magazines, books, airplanes, rockets, etc.

One reason why this communication system is vitally important to us is that for some time we have been using it to monitor globally the changes in the natural environment, have already created an enormous data bank, and have been using it to help resolve interrelated eco-problems. However, we have not yet been responding sufficiently to our guiding information. We must respond, because Nature is telling us to take care of Earth or we will send ourselves to join the dinosaurs. In the US we have not been paying enough attention to the warnings, because we have been told that we can not afford to, that "we need to continue to use our planet's natural resources at our present rate "in order to keep the economy going." Obviously this type of economy can not be sustained.

Another reason why we need the global communication system is to help us recover from our unfounded fears and recognize the real problems we need to fear and resolve: climate change, war, over-population, disease, famine, and political and economic systems that do not respond adequately to the needs of the citizens. We need to continue to develop and share the information and technology which help us to become aware of these common human enemies, and how to fight and defeat them.

Perhaps most importantly, we need to share the information which helps us to see that Natural Law is the non-manmade, impartial, universally accepted, incorruptible guide we need, because we can all *trust* it. In terms of it we can build the interpersonal trust and morality necessary to creating democratic governments locally and globally, and through these we can form and carry out the necessary global democratic plans of action.

However, the "incorruptible" natural guide can remain so only if we do not invade it. Very unfortunately, we have for some time been invading it through overly controlling and destroying our life-sustaining natural environment. We recognize this now, and are working to correct these actions. However, there is a new invader called "genetically modified organisms" (GMOs), a quantum jump which has enabled us to totally change the natural process of food growing. In order to protect consumers, some 60 nations now require labeling of all products containing GMOs.

It is *essential* that we recognize our need for our natural guide, and our need to retain its natural workings. If we are to have any kind of "Genetic Engineering" (GE), we must put tight controls on it. Experts who know the most about it are terrified of what horrors it can produce (and may have already produced) even with controls put on it. If we do continue to pursue it, any ways in which it is altering the workings of our natural guide must be made public so that the alterations can be understood and offset.

To summarize: Today it has become clear that as food-producers we have attempted unsuccessfully to ignore the Laws of Nature and consequently are suffering greatly, those in power and those under them. The results are for all individual persons to be disenfranchised and to become slaves to a monster of their own creation... an anti-Nature, anti-human, anti-individual, Dark Culture which has been spawned by anti-Nature, anti-human, anti-individual governmental/economic systems. These cannot be trusted, and must be abandoned.

To build our fourth human paradise we must be able to trust each other, which means we must be able to believe that our system of government will guarantee our personal rights and enable us to prevent the rise of tyrants. That is why the plan for the government of our communities, from local to global, must be based on the vital needs of the individual person, and on the recognition of the dependence of all of us on the workings of our ecosystem, and on our understanding of why these workings must be monitored by a democratically conceived and operated global observation and communication system which we will all use to guide us.

In regard to our needs as individual persons, what we each need and desire is to be part of a cooperative social system in which we each participate so that we can be in charge of our own lives. For centuries we have invented theories and arguments about what kind of governmental and economic systems would best serve us, and in modern times the basic issue has been about whether our systems should be unplanned or planned. This is a very bad joke because our human systems have always been planned, and by human minds. The only real issue is, which human minds will do the planning? The only viable answer is: The minds of everyone. We have learned for certain that to be successful we must govern ourselves through democracy.

Clearly we need the natural guide and global communication system not only to promote personal awareness and trust, but to help us recover from our unfounded fears and to help us recognize what we really need to fear, including overpopulation, war, disease, the destruction of our natural life-support system, and incompetent human governmental systems. Therefore we need to continue to develop and share the information and technology which help us toward our goals, and we need model communities to inspire and guide us. Even if we can not all for awhile live in model communities, we need to design them, and to apply as much of the designs as we can to our existing communities.

Chapter 11
Mountain Meadows

For many years I had desired to live in an "Intentional Community" but did not take the step because of my concern about my nervousness. But I gradually recovered and as "Senior Citizens" my wife and I discovered, not precisely an "IC," but something similar that was appropriate to our advanced ages and amazingly affordable: "Mountain Meadows," a retirement community for 55 and over persons, high on a hill just inside Ashland, Oregon's city limits, "A place you do not have to move from as you age."

The idea for it came from a lady named Madeline Hill, who with her husband Hunter bought the 22 acre property in 1989 and began construction in 1995. For about 10 years before building Mountain Meadows she attended senior potlucks at churches, meetings of retired educators and neighborhood groups, and asked these people what they would like in an ideal retirement community. She also attended conferences and visited many retirement communities to look around and interview residents and administrators.

When she retired she worked with professionals to design the site plan and structures, get the permits and funding, and begin the work. "Mountain Meadows" opened in 1997 and now has three large buildings with condo apartments and many condo houses, and the grounds are beautiful. It is a friendly, cooperative community and for many reasons we love living here, including that there is a large, beautiful dining room serving delicious healthful meals, a fitness center with swimming pool, our own raised-bed vegetable garden, and the community is run by a mixture of professional staff and various democratically elected resident-boards. The total number of persons living here averages 367 persons.

We have lived here four years and have enjoyed it immensely.

Chapter 12
Cooperatives

In addition to the millions of years of pre-agricultural cooperative groups there is a long history of post-agricultural ones. In the US today there are many thousands of them of every kind... credit unions, bakeries, groceries, childcare, etc., etc.

The business aspect of the movement may have begun in early China where it was a custom for men to undertake a journey to a sacred mountain at least once during a lifetime, and to defray the cost of a pilgrimage credit or savings societies were founded. Through the centuries, around the world there have been many other examples such as irrigation coops, construction coops, food coops, and others.

One of the first known business cooperatives in the U.S. was founded in 1752 by Benjamin Franklin. Called the "Philadelphia Contributorship for the Insurance of Houses from Loss by Fire," it is the oldest continuing cooperative in the U.S.

Some of the earliest attempts to conduct business on a cooperative basis in Britain occurred around 1760, when dockworkers in Woolwich and Chatham established their own grain mills to curb the monopolistic practices of millers. In 1769 a small group of weavers in Ayrshire, Scotland, began a business venture on a cooperative basis. They formed a group to purchase supplies for handicraft production, including weaver's reeds, and also purchased consumer goods for resale, including flour, sugar, and oatmeal.

In 1793 the British Parliament passed an act that assured the people the right to invest capital to form voluntary associations to aid one another during times of sickness, need, and bereavement. By 1800 there were in the British Kingdom 7,200 of these, called "Friendly Societies," with a membership of 600 thousand.

In 1799 Robert Owen was part owner and head of the Lanark cotton mills in Scotland. He improved conditions for workers and their families and pioneered in cooperative and trades unions movements in Britain and in the U.S.

Inspired by these and other ventures, a group of 28 persons in the small industrial town of Rochdale, England, conceived the ideas which became the foundation for the modern business cooperative movement. Mostly flannel weavers, they named themselves the "Rochdale Society of Equitable Pioneers," and on December 21, 1844 they opened a small grocery store on Toad Lane. Each put a pound sterling into a fund to rent the store and purchase flour, sugar, butter, and oatmeal at wholesale prices. They sold food at current prices, for cash, and distributed the savings periodically to members on the basis of patronage. Each member had a single vote in management regardless of the number of shares owned.

The *ideas* created in this small store by 28 persons now serve hundreds of millions of persons living in almost every nation. They called their organizational and working rules and practices the "Principles of Cooperation." In addition to one vote per person, the Rochdale Principles included open membership, democratic control, no religious or political discrimination, sales at prevailing market prices, and the setting aside of some earnings for education. This cooperative, democratic, business contract restored trust in human relationships, and their store grew until its membership totaled over 45,000 persons and its capital over half a million pounds.

The cooperative movement developed rapidly in the latter part of the 19th Century, particularly in the industrial and mining areas of northern Britain and Scotland. It spread quickly among the urban working class in Britain, France, Germany, and Sweden and among the rural population of Norway, The Netherlands, Denmark, and Finland. Cooperatives were introduced in Latin America by European immigrants in the early 1900s, and later were often fostered by state action in connection with agrarian reform.

In the U.S. a cooperative creamery was built at Goshen, Connecticut in 1810. Following this event a number of cheese rings and cooperative dairies were organized in eastern states and later in Wisconsin and other Midwestern states. In 1865 Michigan passed what is believed to be the first law recognizing the cooperative method of buying and selling. The National Grange and Farmers' Alliance promoted cooperatives, and by 1890 farmers had about 1,000 cooperatives. The Farmers Educational and Cooperative Union, founded in 1901, The Cooperative League, founded in 1916 (now known as the National Cooperative Business Association, Wash., D.C.), and The American Farm Bureau Federation, founded in 1919, have supported cooperation.

The period of most intensive growth in number of cooperative associations in the U.S. extended from 1915 to 1930, mainly because of a transition in legal status; cooperatives were placed under statute laws rather than common law. Many states passed enabling laws in this period. In 1922 Congress enacted the Capper-Volstead Act allowing farmers to act together to market their products without being in violation of antitrust laws. The act provided that such associations must be democratically controlled by their members and that they either limit dividends on capital stock issues to 8 percent annually or not deal in the products of nonmembers in amounts greater in value than such as are handled for members.

Later, Congress established governmental agencies to provide loans and assistance to cooperatives, in 1929 the Farm Credit Administration, in 1934 the National Credit Union Administration, and in 1936 the Rural Electrification Administration. In 1978 Congress passed the National Consumer Cooperative Bank Act, establishing the National Cooperative Bank. The National Council of Farmer Cooperatives is located in Washington, D.C., as is also the headquarters of The Farmer Cooperative Service of the U.S. Dept. of Agriculture.

In the U.S. today over 100 million people are members of some 47 thousand cooperatives, such as consumer, artist, agricultural, housing, education, information, communication, transportation, investment, bank, bakery, childcare, credit union, and so on.

Every place on Earth where people have been allowed to establish free institutions, cooperatives have appeared. They work together on the local, regional, national, and international levels to promote exchange among cooperatives, foster cooperative development, provide educational services and provide a forum for examining and acting on common concerns for cooperatives. Numerous cooperative associations throughout the United States provide industry-specific services, educational programs, and financial and other services to their member cooperatives.

At the global level there is the International Cooperative Alliance (ICA), an independent, non- governmental association which unites, represents and serves cooperatives worldwide. Its members are national and international cooperative organizations in all sectors of activity including agriculture, banking, energy, industry, insurance, fisheries, housing, tourism, and consumer needs. Founded in London in August of 1895, the ICA now has over 230 member organizations in over 100 countries, representing more than 730 million individuals worldwide, serving half of the world's population in all sectors of the economy. Its Head Office is in Geneva, Switzerland, website: coop.org/ica.

The main objective of the ICA is to promote and strengthen autonomous cooperatives throughout the world. Through actions taken at the international, regional, and national levels the ICA seeks also to:

- promote and protect cooperative values and principles;
- facilitate the development of economic and other mutually beneficial relations between its member organizations;
- further the economic and social progress of its members and their communities.

In order to achieve its aims, the ICA organizes international, regional, and sectorial meetings, thus serving as a forum for the exchange of experience and information among its vast membership. The original Rochdale Principles have been amended over the years but remain basically the same and are now known worldwide as the "Principles of the International Cooperative Alliance." They are:

1. Membership of a cooperative society should be voluntary and without artificial restriction or any social, political, racial or religious discrimination, to all persons who can make use of its services and are willing to accept the responsibilities of membership.

2. Cooperative societies are democratic organizations. Their affairs should be administered by persons elected or appointed in a manner agreed to by the members and accountable to them. Members of primary societies should enjoy equal rights of voting (one member, one vote) and participation in decisions affecting their societies. In other than primary societies the administration should be conducted on a democratic basis in a suitable form.
3. Share capital should only receive a strictly limited rate of interest.
4. The economic results arising out of the operations of a society belong to the members of that society and should be distributed in such a manner as would avoid one member gaining at the expense of others. This may be done by decision of the members as follows: (a) by provision for development of the business of the cooperative; (b) by provision of common services; or (c) by distribution among members in proportion to their transactions with the society.
5. All cooperative societies should make provision for the education of their members, officers, and employees and of the general public in the principles and techniques of cooperation, both economic and democratic.
6. All cooperative organizations, in order to best serve the interest of their members and their communities, should actively cooperate in every practical way with other cooperatives at local, national, and international levels.

The foregoing is a very small part of the history of cooperatives, and is intended only to indicate its direction and long, slow-but-steady struggle and progress. Fortunately there is a vast store of information on the subject in public libraries, online, etc.

In addition to the ICA, two other important contributors have been: "The Fellowship for Intentional Community" (FIC), and the work of the late W. Edwards Deming. We will begin with the FIC.

The FIC website (ic.org) states that "Intentional Communities" (ICs) is an inclusive term for ecovillages, cohousing, residential land trusts, communes, student coops, urban housing coops, and other related projects. To promote awareness of ICs and cooperation among them and among all persons on Earth, the FIC was formed in 1948 in Yellow

Springs, Ohio. The 2005 edition of the FIC "Communities Directory" describes over 700 ICs in North America and around the world, alternative resources and services, and many articles about community living. The 30 year old FIC quarterly magazine, "Communities: Journal of Cooperative Living," has published numerous descriptive articles by persons living in ICs. This information is extremely helpful to other persons living in ICs, and to persons looking for an IC to visit and possibly to join. The Journal and the "Newsletter" update information on all aspects of global community topics.

As we have seen, the actual history of ICs began when a small group of early humans intentionally changed their individual thinking and behavior in order to function more cooperatively as a coordinated group, thereby enormously helping themselves to survive and to enjoy being alive. Today's ICs strive to emulate this success, and what they have done, learned, and recorded provides us now with desperately needed information.

From ICs, which are community and in varying degrees business oriented, we can proceed to the specifically business oriented work of W. Edwards Deming (1900-1992). During WW II he introduced methods of quality control in U.S. factories which greatly improved production of vital military equipment. As a result of these quality control achievements he was assigned in 1950 by the Allied Supreme Command in Tokyo as an adviser in sampling techniques to help rebuild war-torn Japan.

Invited by the members of the Union of Japanese Scientists and Engineers to teach them his statistical methods of quality control, he conducted a series of eight-day seminars throughout the nation. Among other things he told Japanese business leaders to ignore American business techniques and avoid pitting management against labor or one department against another or even one worker against another. Cooperation, not competition, he said, is the key to industrial success. Merit pay, which had long been a staple in American plants, destroyed worker morale. Quota systems were equally counter-productive because the pressure to meet them led workers to sacrifice quality in their rush to make their numbers. Inspection at the end of the line, which had been the traditional anchor of quality control in

American manufacturing, only made it easier to expect defects. Far better, he said, to eliminate defects as they occur, at various points in the production process.

In short, he recommended that the Japanese manage the system of production, not the people who make it work. His fundamental idea is to think of an organization as a total system, wherein each part, each person, is as important as the others. The first step is to decide your purpose, your long term aim. What are you doing? Why? His program comprises 14 points to improve quality, each of which is vital to the whole. His business philosophy focuses on cooperation and continual improvement in people, processes, and systems. The Japanese credit him with teaching them how to produce better quality goods and services with less effort and materials. He was so revered in Japan that the emperor bestowed the country's highest honor on him.

Even as Japanese industry prospered under Deming's influence throughout the 1960s and '70s, reaching an annual growth rate of 11 percent by 1980, American industry largely ignored him. All that changed on June 24, 1980, when NBC aired a ninety-minute documentary, "If Japan Can, Why Can't We?" that spotlighted Deming's role in the rise of Japanese industry. Subsequently Deming was besieged by American companies, and signed consulting contracts with both Ford and GM, two companies reeling under Japanese competition, as well as with Florida Power & Light, Dow Chemical, Hughes Aircraft, and others. Subsequently he received many high honors for his brilliant successes with businesses, the Federal Government, schools, hospitals, etc.

Including additional comments Deming made during the TV documentary in 1980, Deming's 14 points are:

1. Create constancy of purpose for improvement. (With a long view of staying in business and creating more and more jobs rather than making money quickly.)
2. Refuse to accept poor workmanship or negative attitudes. (Everybody wins. Cooperation is to everyone's benefit.)
3. Eliminate the end-of-the-line inspection, and work on correcting defects at the source. (Design quality into the product, rather than costly inspecting and fixing later.)

4. Avoid awarding contracts based on price alone; seek out and stick with quality vendors. (Don't buy on price tag alone.)
5. Strive continually to improve production and service.
6. Develop formal worker training programs. (Training for skills. Only people can create change and make improvements.)
7. Urge supervisors to practice leadership by example. (You can not delegate quality; it must come from motivated persons.)
8. Let workers know that questions are welcome. (Drive out fear, build trust; "strict control" doesn't work. The need is to please the customer, not the boss.)
9. Stress cooperation, not competition, among departments. (Break down borders, barriers. Everyone wins, no one loses. Everything is a system. Contribution, not competition.)
10. Encourage workers to come up with their own slogans.
11. Abolish quotas. (The method is what is important, the way you do it. Eliminate goals.)
12. Make it possible for employees to take pride in their work by ensuring that equipment and supplies are in optimum condition. (Joy in work. Remove barriers. Abolish merit system. Don't grade students. One cannot enjoy doing something if doing it only to beat someone else.)
13. Educate and retrain both management and workers. (Continuing education, not only about the job but about other subjects.)
14. Form a special management team with a plan to carry out the quality mission. (To accomplish the transformation must get everybody committed, not just a few. Everybody wins, cooperation is to everyone's benefit.)

To achieve communication, personal participation, trust, responsibility, and commitment, workers were organized into small groups (teams) representing steps in the production process.

In Deming's view American business leaders were wrong to blame the American trade deficit on Japan or on American workers. He said that the cause of the decline in American productivity is that management have walked off the job of management, striving instead for dividends and good performance of the price of the company's stock. A better way to serve stockholders would be to stay in business with constant improvement of quality of product and of service, thus to decrease costs, capture markets, provide jobs, and increase dividends. Failure of management to plan for the future and to foresee problems has brought about waste of manpower, of materials, and of machine time, all of which raise the manufacturer's cost and the price that the purchaser must pay. The consumer is not always willing to subsidize this waste. The inevitable result is loss of market. Loss of market begets unemployment. Performance of management should be measured by potential to stay in business, to protect investment, to ensure future dividends and jobs through improvement of product and service for the future, not by the quarterly dividend. It is no longer socially acceptable to dump employees on to the heap of unemployed. Loss of market, and resulting unemployment, are not foreordained. They are not inevitable. They are manmade. The basic cause of sickness in American industry and resulting unemployment is the failure of top management to manage. In Deming's view the purpose of all management, the purpose of cooperation, is to bring out the best in each person and allow each person to contribute fully. (Fourth brain ideas.)

Chapter 13
Mondragon

NOTE: For up to date information go to their website at: mondragon-corporation.com.

The Mondragon System is the most widely known and studied cooperative system on Earth. It has been tested for half a century and has proved to be a successful concept. A fundamental reason for its success is that it copies the essential parts of the original human cooperative, and does so in a way which enables us to continue to produce food.

Founded in 1956 in the Basque region of northern Spain, the model for the system has grown from a five member worker-owned and managed coop manufacturing kerosene kitchen stoves, to a group of 160 interrelated coops with over 23,000 workers, annual sales of over $6 billion, and assets of over $11 billion. The coops are industrially based, financially sound, and surplus sharing, and engage in finance, production (80 %), distribution, and services. It offers cooperative schools, housing, health, and other services, and has some 100 thousand associates in its consumer cooperative retail stores. (For the full story see "From Mondragon to America," by Greg MacLeod, University College of Cape Breton Press, Sydney, Nova Scotia, Canada 1997)

Our story leads directly to it as being a means to put ourselves back on our successful course, because it has re-invented the idea of being human and has created a situation in which the idea has been put into practice. The participants in the system have been motivated and able to become not only consciously cooperative, but highly successful industrially, economically, governmentally, socially, and educationally, thereby re-creating the essential elements of the original human situation, including the re-creation of an "in" for everyone to be in.

One way this was accomplished was by stopping the growth of the original cooperative at the number of persons appropriate to having an optimum social and business community, i.e. large enough for persons to meet their physical, mental, social, and economic needs, and small enough to be democratic. Instead of letting the first coop become too large, a second coop was created, and then a third, and a fourth, until now there are around 160 coops, each self-governing but all linked together so as to be able to assist each other and the whole. As noted, there are now some 23 thousand worker-owners, total annual sales are over $6 billion, and assets are over $11 billion.

The model for the system is called "The Mondragon Cooperatives," and is located in the small town of Mondragon in the Basque region of northern Spain. A quote from their website is: "Mondragon Corporacion Cooperativa (MCC) is a unique experience in development through cooperation in the world. Over the last 40 years MCC has based its success, in both business and social terms, on industrial democracy, participation, and solidarity. The main feature of the Mondragon cooperatives is that their workers are also members and the owners of their companies. The cooperatives are managed democratically on a one-person, one-vote basis."

Another main feature of the coops is that there is no unemployment. When market conditions warrant downsizing of a coop persons are shifted to another one. They take their benefits with them, and if need be are retrained. Its design is intended to meet the human needs of each person on Earth, in that it is democratic, worker-owned and managed, creates employment for everyone, meets their economic needs, and prevents anyone from gaining personal power. The system rejects communism, socialism, fascism, and mainstream so-called "capitalism," which for several reasons is not capitalism at all, three reasons being that it is monopolistic, undemocratic, and destroys the markets and capital on which it depends, i.e. people and their life-sustaining natural resources.

In contrast to this the Mondragon system is private enterprise in a fair and viable "capitalist" form, in that persons invest money to become worker-owners of the companies, and the companies participate in the so-called free market system and rely on it for the setting of prices.

But it is different in that owners must be workers, and each one has only one vote regardless of the amount of money he or she invests. This is in stark contrast to companies owned by absentee stockholders whose goal is to make the maximum return on their investment in the shortest time, without regard for the well-being of others. Also the system rejects the arrogant, unfair, dehumanizing practice of giving managers (e.g. CEOs) huge salaries, stock options, etc. At the same time the cooperative system recognizes that highly trained and skilled managers are needed to handle the complex decisions of a large company in the post-industrial world, and that their services require a higher rate of compensation. But to protect against inequities the highest paid persons can receive no more than six times that of the *lowest* paid person. By comparison, as a group top managers in the US receive 185 times their *average* employee's pay, through salaries, bonuses, stock options, etc. Also they may not feel personal loyalty to their employees or investors and sometimes become super rich by selling out and leaving employees and investors with nothing, e.g. ENRON and WorldCom.

Clearly the Mondragon Cooperatives constitute a sound, practical, successful, worker-owned and managed, non-sectarian, non-political, cooperative, business system which meets the educational, industrial, economic, financial, and democratic organizational needs of its individual participants, thereby creating the necessary foundation for them to meet their health, financial, and social needs. Its principles include the basic principles of the International Cooperative Alliance (ICA), but go further.

The fundamental way in which this new industrial/economic/ financial/ social system is like the original human one, and unlike the prevailing one, is that it was created by individual persons to enable each one of them to meet his or basic human needs, and to do so in ways which enable others to meet theirs.

The Mondragon system's mentor was Don Jose Maria Arrizmendiarrieta, "Don" being a title of respect bestowed on him by his associates. He lived from 1915 to 1976, and I regret that I did not begin to become aware of his life and work while he was alive.

He and I were each motivated to work for peace and social justice because of having been in a war. He fought the Spanish fascists who were led by the bloody dictator Franco in their rebellion against the Spanish Republic from 1936 to 1939, and I fought the German fascists (Nazis) who were led by the bloody dictator Hitler in the Second World War which went from 1939 to 1945. Because the Spanish fascists received enormous and decisive military aid from the German fascists, and from the Italian fascists led by the bloody dictator Mussolini, WW II was actually the continuation of the Spanish Civil War. The foreign fascists used the war to test their new weapons and tactics.

When war broke out in 1936 Don Jose interrupted his studies for the priesthood to join the Basque army and fight along with the other citizens of the duly-elected Spanish Republic against the unelected Spanish military invader, General Franco. During that terrible, murderous war Don Jose saw cities and their inhabitants destroyed by flights of fascist bombers. In 1937 Pablo Picasso did his famous painting, *Guernica,* as a protest against the destruction by Nazi bombers of the town of that name which was the ancient capital of the Basque country. Don Jose saw the volunteers from Spain and other nations fight desperately and courageously to save the Republic and their freedom, and saw them slaughtered by German and Italian bombs and guns. He saw that no amount of courage, will, and stamina could succeed against superior technology.

After the fascist victory in 1939 Don Jose was put into one of Franco's concentration camps and sentenced to death, but through an error he escaped execution. Later he was ordained a priest and sent to the town of Mondragon.

In the social hierarchy of Spain the people were either very rich and powerful, or very poor and powerless, and this is the situation which Don Jose desired to change. He set out to help the poor and unemployed persons have work that would enable them to live decent lives. Because of his war experience he saw that to succeed in modern times they would need to be educated in technology.

Therefore in 1943, as assistant pastor in the local church, with monetary help from citizens of the town he organized a technical school. Through the years it has grown to become the Polytechnic University, the continuing source of training and research for what became the Mondragon Cooperatives. Today the "Eskola Politeknika" has an enrollment of some 2,000 students and is considered the best technical institute in Spain and one of the best anywhere.

In 1956 five of his students returned from university and with his help set up a cooperative kitchen stove factory which met their goals of being community based, effectively democratic, non-sectarian, worker-owned and managed, financially sound, and surplus sharing. Originally it was named ULGOR, after a letter in the name of each of the five founders, but to make the name represent its present activity it is now called Fagor Electrodomesticos.

As more persons invested money in the business and became worker-owners and managers ULGOR grew quickly in size and was so successful that after three years the five young founders and Don Jose desired to create employment for other needy persons. From the disastrous experiences of previous cooperatives they recognized that for continuing success ULGOR must be kept small enough to be democratic, and that rather than enlarging its membership the appropriate course would be to create another cooperative.

They knew also that in Europe many cooperatives had failed over the years because traditional private banks were not prepared to support them in difficult times. As they could not depend on financial assistance from Franco's Madrid (he was dictator until his death in 1975), the second cooperative they created was a credit union so that the Basque people could put their capital into industry in the Basque region rather than sending it to a bank in Madrid. This helped to stop the flight of capital out of the Basque region. It helped also to stop the outmigration of young persons, because new employment opportunities were created by using the money invested in the Caja to start a third cooperative business, and then a fourth, and so on, each of which met the original standards.

Today the credit union, called the "Caja Laboral Popular," has been rated as among the 100 most efficient financial institutions in the world in terms of its profit/asset ratio. With 125 branches under one board and one general manager the Caja has become very effective in attracting savings from the local area. If their own banking system had not been created the Mondragon cooperative system could not have been successful.

Some of the pro-Franco, conservative Church leaders criticized Don Jose for promoting the creation of additional cooperatives, but he continued to because he saw the establishment of new economic structures as the only means for the Basque people to survive.

Some persons said that a business based on personal values could not survive, but Don Jose proved this to be untrue. He said, "The economic revolution will be moral or it will not succeed; the moral revolution will be economic or it will not succeed." He opposed state socialism, charging that in traditional capitalism capital held the power over the worker, while in state socialism the state bureaucracy held the power over the worker. He opposed violent revolution, saying that a system put in place through force would always require force to maintain it. After analyzing all economic systems he decided that the free market system was the best one for the setting of prices.

By creating more cooperatives the founders avoided another error which had proved fatal to so many cooperatives, that of being isolationist and marginal in the overall economy. In an organic fashion new branches have been developed in new types of industry, economics, finance, services, etc., and then branches of the branches, regionally, nationally, and globally, yet the interlinkages have been maintained.

Because of its success "the Mondragon experiment," as it is known worldwide, is under study by numerous governments, trade unions, and social scientists. It is proof that worker-owned and managed cooperatives can flourish and constitute a major part of a nation's economy and also participate in the economies of other nations.

. . . . .

At this point it is necessary to recognize that our basic interest in this book is in the Mondragon *system*. Of course we are interested in the Mondragon *model* (MCC), because it has been the model for the system.

However, the unfortunate present problem for MCC is that in order to survive it has had to expand into the growing international economy, and to do so MCC has had in some ways to deviate from its original standards or disappear altogether. Some examples are: the MCC model has had to hire temporary workers who were not made members; MCC can not organize democratic factories in England or the U.S., so they simply buy subsidiaries, sometimes in strategic partnerships with other corporations; MCC will accept contracts to produce components for large traditionally capitalist corporations like General Electric. So the problem is not with the Mondragon system, but with the inhuman systems and practices in the rest of the world. For example, the giant global corporations search the world over to find places to locate their factories where workers receive the lowest pay, work the longest hours, and have no benefits or unions.

The model has proved that the Mondragon System can function in conjunction with the existing regional, national, and international business systems, and that if the Mondragon system were expanded as we need it to be it could replace non-cooperative systems without there being a loss in production, distribution, jobs, income, or services. This is the first cooperative business system to have demonstrated this capability, and that is a main reason why its continuing existence and expansion are so vitally important to us.

In addition to the above, it is important to note that in recent years the Italian coop movement has become even larger than the Basque, with about 250,000 worker coop members. This is partly because the Italian constitution recognizes the role of coops in job creation and directs that legislation should promote them, so the law gives them favorable tax status.

. . . . .

Thus far in this chapter we can see several reasons why our human story leads directly to the creation of the Mondragon system as the means to regain our successful course by meeting the requirements of a formula: Wherever food production has had negative side effects we must find positive ways to offset them.

The Mondragon system follows the formula because it is designed to make it not only possible, but desirable and rewarding, for persons to establish trust and cooperation within their groups. This is achieved by keeping the groups small enough for their members to see each other on a recurring basis and to participate personally in the decision-making process. This corrects one mistake made by our food-producing ancestors, which was to cause the breakdown of trust and cooperation within groups by letting them become too large.

In the Mondragon system no one can gain personal power over anyone else. As we have seen, in the pre-agricultural groups one could not gain personal power for three main reasons: people depended on the natural food-producing system for their sustenance, and as they did not create the system, and did not have to maintain it, there were no work assignments to be forced on persons; because no one could control the system, no one could use it to control other persons; persons could see that they desperately needed the voluntary help of other persons, and that because this could not be forced it had to be earned.

In the Mondragon system it is recognized that there must be skilled managers who have acquired the necessary education and that they are entitled to a reasonably higher rate of pay. However the system provides everyone with a basic education and the opportunity to go on to higher education, all positions are open to those who can meet the requirements, and the General Assembly votes to seat or to unseat any official by a majority vote. This also corrects a part of the second mistake made by our ancestors, which was to allow a few persons to gain control of the production and distribution of the food supply and enslave everyone else, which also meant to enslave themselves.

The Mondragon system is consciously and purposefully built on a cooperative, democratic, industrial base, so that it can not be manipulated. Out of it comes economic and political democracy and social justice. An essential factor of the system is that the decision-making process has been designed to accommodate the work schedules of each person.

The first mistake of our early human ancestors was not to be able to continue to build trust and cooperation between groups. The Mondragon system makes it not only possible, but desirable and rewarding for an unlimited number of groups of persons to trust and to cooperate with each other.

It must be emphasized that our ancestors could not have avoided either the first or the second mistake, because they did not have the necessary information. We do have it, and it is our task today to use it to achieve what they could not.

We can see that the system restores the effects of two of the original motivating elements of the natural environment, i.e. small groups, and the sharing, not of food itself, but of the money necessary to buy it. It does make food sharing possible because of the cooperative neighborhood philosophy. Also, the MCC Distribution Group includes five co-ops involved in food systems.

In a recent Mondragon publication a cooperative model was compared to a traditional capitalist model. Of the ten comparisons given, the first two are:

Co-op: Priority of persons, professionalism, excellence of products, satisfaction of clients.

Cap: Priority of the financial, meaning the highest and most rapid return on investment.

Co-op: Persons form part of the enterprise. They are part of the purpose and participate in management.

Cap: Persons are considered as means and are expendable.

Thus the vital difference between the two systems is in their *objective*. The Mondragon system exists to benefit its workers and everyone else, and the traditional capitalist system exists to make money for a few persons regardless of the effects on anyone.

This does not mean that capitalist/corporative companies do not try to provide for the well-being of their workers and everyone else; in various ways most, if not all, do try. However, this is not their *objective*, and they sometimes fire workers not to make a reasonable amount of money, but to make as much money as is possible, regardless of how many employees and their families lose their livelihood. This practice does not really make sense because businesses need customers, and if the workers have no income they can not afford to buy. It is a result of the tradition of "laissez faire" economics, which took "the blind forces of the market" for its guide.

By way of comparison, the Basque region lost well over 100,000 jobs during Spain's deep ten-year recession that began in 1975, yet during that difficult time Mondragon coops actually added workers. In addition to Mondragon's own website there are several other sites relating to Mondragon Corporation which are listed on the same page. As these can be visited on computers in homes or in public libraries we need not go further into their content here.

Clearly, the ideas in the Mondragon system contribute to the spirit of the fourth human paradise.

Note: As already noted, for up to date information see website Mondragon.

Chapter 14
Peak Oil

As we are all learning from the experts, the term "peak oil" does not mean that we are about to run out of oil. Rather it refers to the point at which oil production begins to decline, and our problem is that we have become so dependent on cheap, abundant fossil fuels – coal, natural gas, and especially oil – that we are not prepared to have less of them each year rather than more.

Oil is the most energy-dense and convenient fuel to use, so more than 90 percent of the world's transportation is fueled by oil, and in the US it is close to 100 percent. So oil is not something that is easy to replace, when worldwide we are using about 85 million barrels a day.

Over the decades individual oil wells and oil fields have gone into terminal decline, and there has been declining oil production in whole nations, starting with the US in 1970. Since then around 30 other countries have gone into oil production decline. This will eventually occur for the world as a whole, though there is some dispute as to exactly when it will happen. Some persons say it already happened in 2005. Others say it will not be until sometime in the 2030's. But everyone agrees that it will happen during the lifetimes of most persons living today. People who are personally surveying the oil fields say it will occur within the next four years.

It can seem that the start of the decline would not be a problem, because it would seem that oil supplies would taper off gradually. But the problem does begin with the start of the decline, because we have created an industrial economy based on growth, and a certain percentage of growth is needed each year to prevent economic collapse. So when transportation becomes more expensive and it becomes clear that this is not just a temporary problem of supply and demand, it will lead to panic. The relentless decline in availability of fuel will cause a crisis unlike any we have seen in the history of the industrial or information ages.

For example, in the US almost our entire food system depends on the use of oil to run machinery to raise food and to transport it in trucks, airplanes, trains, and ships, and to run autos; natural gas is used abundantly in the food and other industries and in homes; and both are used to generate the electricity which is involved in running almost everything.

The shortages which occurred on the home front here in America and in Australia during World War II were only a tiny indication of the crisis that is coming. During that war food, gasoline, and other items needed for the military were rationed and people raised food at home in Victory Gardens. In Europe and Asia shortages in most countries involved in the war were incomparably worse. But even those shortages were temporary, and the coming shortages and their terrible effects will be permanent, unless we humans make the necessary changes in the ways we think and live.

To see a modern-day example of human reaction to impending crisis we can refer to the recent incident called "Y2K" (Year 2000). In the US all of our vital systems are run by computers, and during the month before the year 2000 began there was a great fear that they would crash because their dating systems might not handle the double zeros. People began to store food, water, and gasoline, buy electricity generators, lanterns, and other survival items, and, most importantly, began to talk to their neighbors about making cooperative plans to prepare for emergency transportation, etc. However, because of an all out cooperative effort by computer experts the computers did not fail, people lost the fear which had motivated them, returned to over-consuming our natural resources as fast as possible, and forgot about cooperation and community.

Nevertheless, this immediate, cooperative response to expected calamity shows two vital facts: that though our situation changes, we remain innately prone to be cooperative, and that we can do what we need to when adequately motivated by fear of a common danger.

Since then we have had several serious warnings of how frail our systems are because of the occurrence of natural disasters such as hurricanes, and breakdowns in manmade equipment, such as electrical blackouts, but we considered these to be repairable and continued to live in Fantasyland.

Of course, the energy to run computers also depends on oil, so this time "Y2K" will really happen.

The advertising industry plays a crucial role in how we think and act, and it has trained us to want more and more material possessions. If the public relations techniques currently devoted to persuading us that we need more possessions could be used instead to convince us that we have to change our thinking and behavior in order to survive, it could make a vital difference. During WW II U.S. citizens were persuaded to participate in rationing of fuel, automobile tires, nylon stockings, and other things, because they knew their survival was at stake. The government, the advertising industry, the motion picture industry, and others all cooperated to support the necessary thinking and behavior.

In the case of the early humans, the result of their not continuing to base their ideas on the evolving workings of their natural environment led to the loss of their paradise.

In the case of Y2K, the result of the computer failure not occurring was that we put off facing our real danger for another eight years, and we can see now that this allowed our situation to become worse.

If our planet were not limited in area and in life-sustaining natural resources we might have continued on our self-destructive course indefinitely, or until we destroyed ourselves. But our planet is limited in these, and as individual persons more and more of us are suffering and dying because we have not taken care of our resources. If we continue on our present self-destructive course much longer it will become too late to stop and reverse it. But if we use our new knowledge of our human past immediately and constructively, it will not be too late.

The reason why the decline in availability of fuel is not just a temporary problem is that renewable energy sources will never become able to fully replace fossil fuels. Consequently we can not simply switch from oil to ethanol or hydrogen and continue with business as usual. That is why we need to be investing much more in alternative energies than we are now, and also begin to change our business and citizen practices now to conserve energy.

The history of our situation is that the Industrial Revolution came about because we went from using low-quality energy sources to more-concentrated, higher quality sources: from wood to coal, and then from coal to oil; later we added natural gas and uranium. As we pass the peak of oil production, and then gas production, and then coal production – which will probably also happen in this century -- we will be moving back down the ladder from high-quality energy sources to lower-quality energy sources. This can be done in a cooperative way, so that we will all be living in peaceful, productive communities, but it will not be an easy transition. It will mean cutting back on many luxuries that we have become accustomed to, such as cheap transportation and moving goods around the planet at great speeds.

The Stone Age ended because humans developed agriculture, and then harnessed animal energy. Any fundamental changes we have experienced since then have involved harvesting more energy from the environment. Now we are going to be extracting less energy, because no new source will give us as much return for the dollar as oil. We can not *replace* our way out of the problem, so we must *conserve* our way out of it, because we have no other choice.

Experts say that some great oil discoveries will be made, but say the problem is that the scale of new discoveries has been declining for the last 40 years. Since the 1950's we have been finding smaller and smaller fields. We did make some big discoveries in central Asia and Iran in 1999 and 2000, but even those are relatively small compared to what we were finding back in the first half of the twentieth century.

But suppose we found ten new Saudi Arabias – and the US Geological Survey is assuming that we will discover several – our consumption is still growing. If it grows at 3.5 percent a year, that means that consumption will double in about 40 years. So even if we make some enormous discoveries, we will still reach a peak ten or twenty years from now.

Several promising renewable energy sources are being developed, and though they help provide energy, none will even come near to replacing oil and natural gas.

So we need to undergo a cultural change. But can we? As we have seen in previous chapters, cultural change has occurred at the level of our relationship with the natural world, particularly in how we get our food. That is why the change from hunter/gatherer to farmer brought such a radical change in our Human Story. Cultural change can happen also at the level of politics, ideology, or religion, but the really fundamental change starts with our relationship to the natural world. Anthropologists call this the cultural infrastructure, as distinct from a society's structure of politics and economics, and superstructure of ideology and religion.

We are on the verge of an infrastructural shift on the scale of the Industrial Revolution. Actually we are going to be experiencing the other side of that revolution, and it will change our political system, our ideologies, and our beliefs. The most important work we can do right now is at the level of infrastructure: finding new ways to meet our basic needs, particularly for food, in a sustainable way.

What we are now learning from experience is that if we have more energy, we can create a more complex society, and that with less energy available, we can not support as high a level of complexity. Hunter/gatherers had access to extremely low-level energy sources, basically food and muscle power, and fire for cooking and heating. Agriculture increased that, and sails, windmills, and water mills increased it more, but not nearly as much as did new fuels. Coal, gas, and oil increased our ability to extract energy from our environment exponentially, enabling the inventions of trains, automobiles, computers, modern cities, and the rest.

As the price of energy rises, people will be thinking about how much oil they are using, and how they are going to get to work, and where their food will come from, and how they will heat and cool their homes.

Cuba went through an energy famine in the 1990's, so Cubans created urban gardens, produced more of their own food, and made more public transportation options available. At the same time, the energy famine did trash the Cuban economy, and our's will be trashed too, because continuing to grow the economy using fossil fuels will not be an option. The question is: Are we going to deal with it in a cooperative way, or in an uncooperative way? Cuba chose the cooperative way and survived.

Until two hundred years ago we had economies which did not have to grow. Since the start of the Industrial Revolution we have created a type of economy that needs to grow, partly because in our U.S. monetary system money is literally loaned into existence by the Federal Reserve. (The system is not all that different in other countries.) The Federal Reserve makes loans to member banks so that they can make loans to commercial customers. So the money that we are using represents debt, as well as promised interest on that debt. The only way that interest can be repaid is if the money supply continues to grow, and a rate of 3 or 4 per cent a year is considered healthy growth. If it slips below that, we have a recession, which means not enough new money is being created to pay back the interest on the existing loans, so people are defaulting on their loans. Money starts disappearing from the system, and it can result in a collapse of the economy such as occurred back in the 1930's during the Great Depression. In our present system, to keep that from happening we have to have continual growth.

In his book, "The Oil Depletion Protocol" (New Society Publishers), Richard Heinberg describes the ODP as being an agreement whereby oil-producing nations would decrease their scale of production - and oil importing nations would decrease the scale of their imports - by 2.6 per cent a year. He chose 2.6 because it is equal to the global oil-depletion rate. He says that if we do not enact the ODP, or a similar plan to reduce consumption, we are going to see extreme price volatility once we pass the peak, and also extreme competition for the oil that can be extracted. He said that we will probably see a World War over control of oil fields. But what the ODP would do is keep prices predictable. They would still be high, but relatively stable, so people, nations, and corporations could plan their economic futures.

Another result of our using fossil fuels for energy is the phenomenon called "global warming." It means that by using fossil fuels we have been sending "greenhouse gas emissions" into the Earth's atmosphere which are causing Earth temperatures to rise. If this continues to occur, ice will continue to melt and raise the sea levels 20 feet, flooding everything with present sea levels below that. Researchers are telling us that to stabilize the world's climate we must cut global warming pollution 25 percent by 2020, and 80 per cent by 2050.

This would require us to make a major adjustment in our way of living, but if we were all to cooperate, we could succeed.

It is now October, 2008, and less than a month to the Presidential and Congressional elections, and there is much talk and planning to make the U.S. independent of foreign oil, and we are moving somewhat in that direction through creation of alternative energy sources, including solar and wind.

Chapter 15
Summary

The success of our human species depends on the success of our human experiment. The success of our human experiment depends on our development of our four-brain reasoning system, and on our using it to create and apply successful, cooperative ideas.

In the human beginning persons had only a three-brain reasoning system. However it was all that was necessary to their success for two reasons. First, because it was developed naturally in each person born, and second because humans lived the natural environment and their reasoning systems were guided by its evolving workings. Consequently persons were able to create successful, cooperative ideas which formed a successful, cooperative, evolving Human Culture.

Eventually, for reasons given previously, this three-brain system was stopped both from developing and evolving. That caused the failure of the Human Experiment and resulted in several thousand years of human destruction of each other, and of their natural environment, a condition which continues to exist today.

Very fortunately, however, some 40 thousand years previously a *fourth* brain had been beginning to emerge in the frontal area of the head, as part of a natural evolutionary sequence of brain emergence. However when third brain development and evolution were stopped, fourth brain development and evolution were also stopped, and broke the evolutionary chain. (A theory is that the next step after the development and integration of the fourth brain, was for it to begin an important dialogue with the brain in our heart, but I have not yet researched this theory.)

This book deals also with an underlying issue which has been my struggle to overcome war- induced PTSD. This has occurred in two periods, which are before and after I was diagnosed in 2003. Before,

I could not know what was wrong with me, and consequently could not know how to deal with it in order to adapt to the workings of the post WW II Culture. After finally being diagnosed, I realized that my primary task was to recover from PTSD, or I would not be able to do anything very well. Surprisingly I found that what I had been doing in researching and writing was helping me so much that it (plus some therapy sessions) was my best way to heal, and the VA psychologists and MD agreed.

Part One of the book tells about my WW II experience, and my subsequent discovery of the work of Julian Huxley. It changed my life and provided the structure for the rest of the book.

Part Two, Our New Human Story, presents what I have had to learn in order to write the book, and at the same time keep overcoming PTSD. It has been very important to my healing to keep my promise to find the origin and cause of war. The book's Conclusion considers our present and future possibilities.

Part Three lists the new ideas which have enabled us to break through the barriers that have kept us from being able to make our Human Experiment again successful.

I got my start by learning from Huxley's book that the Universe is a single Process of Change, called *Evolution,* occurring in three main phases: non-living, living, and human, and that in the human phase the method of evolutionary change is through transmissible Culture. I learned that our Culture consists of the ideas we create to guide our thinking and behavior, and that a "transmissible" Culture could be passed on to each new generation, who would update it to meet the changing and evolving survival requirements of their time.

Therefore what we need to do is create ideas which will enable us to live together in peace and prosperity. Very simple to accomplish in theory, but very difficult in practice. However, it seemed to me that if we could follow the step-by-step Human Story from its beginning into the present time, that would make it possible for persons to accept it as being accurate. Huxley's model plus MacLean's model made it possible for me to see that our Story began when our first human ancestors had inherited a three-brain system which enabled them to reason, and thereby to create cooperative ideas in their minds, and to share them with each other by having developed their potential for vocal language.

What resulted is what I call "The Human Experiment." Its purpose was for persons to see if by using their three part brain reasoning system they could improve their ability to survive and enjoy life by creating and living according to cooperative ideas, rather than having to depend on instinct alone to guide them. Their Experiment was successful, because they studied the evolving workings of their surrounding Natural environment and based their ideas on them. The result was that their ideas, and the Culture these formed, kept evolving, and helped not only them but were passed on and kept evolving and helped new generations, which process was necessary to the continuing success of their Experiment. However, they were not consciously aware of any of the foregoing, even though it was their own accomplishment.

Their Experiment was successful for a long time but then, because of the strong human desire to continually increase their control over their lives, and because they were not aware of the reasons for their success, they changed from using their natural source of ideas, to using an unnatural source (an illogical idea that their lives were ruled by invisible super humans who, because they thought like humans, could be seduced by human praise to help humans). This new source could not evolve, so neither could the ideas nor the Culture that it produced.

From the human beginning their third brain had been the leader, so what was being produced can be called an evolving "third-brain Culture." When the third brain stopped evolving, it lost its ability to function properly as a member of the three-part brain's reasoning system. That caused the system (aka the Human Learning System) to become unable to correct any wrong decisions it was making. That resulted in wrong changes in the human course which were used by humans unknowingly in ways harmful to them.

This brings us to another great scientific breakthrough, which was the discovery that a fourth brain had emerged and had begun to develop some 40 thousand years ago. Its emergence enables us to see that humans had been living in their third-brain Culture far longer than it was capable of helping them, during which time they had needed to be developing their fourth brain and creating a fourth-brain Culture. Instead, during those thousands of years the non-evolving third brain had stagnated and became more and more corrupted by Humans to the point that they were actually causing it to *invite* them to sink to the depths that have been reached today.

Another fact of which we must be aware is that during this time many persons actually did develop their fourth brain, and many of them made wonderful contributions, large or small, to the Human Experiment. However, even though personal contributions are the vital base of the Culture, what we live by is the *great group of ideas*, the great mass of them, which form the total entity we call our Human Culture.

From the human beginning and for many thousands of years our third brain and its Culture had done a great job of enabling humans to evolve and advance, and of preparing them for the development of the fourth brain; then some power-seeking persons stopped that from happening by suppressing new ideas. Now that we can understand all this, we can begin to create the ideas needed to repair the functioning of the three-brain system, so that it can begin to create the ideas needed to continue the development of the fourth brain and its Culture. That will enable us to enter The Fourth Human Paradise by persons cooperating with each other democratically all over our beautiful planet Earth.

However, if we continue to let ignorant, money-mad, power-seeking groups propagandize us and our children into accepting false and destructive ideas about our human past, present, and possible future, we will continue to destroy our natural environment and ourselves.

So it seems that our modern human situation has been a matter of our ability or inability to use reason to become consciously aware of the existence and workings of our Human Experiment. Instead, we used our third brain's period of failure to lead us astray, which prevented our fourth brain from developing sufficiently to assume its proper leadership in a four-brain system.

Thus the question we are facing today is: Has the Experiment been successful? The answer is yes and no.

It was certainly "yes" in the human beginning, because our early ancestors created and shared a cooperative idea which enabled them to defeat the leopard. They had continuing success with their Experiment, and enlarged its use to create ideas relating to more and more ways to improve their lives. However, today the answer to the question must be "no," because power-seeking persons have suppressed cooperative ideas, and that not only killed the Experiment, but took us off of our successful course and put us on the self-destructive course on which we find ourselves today.

Does that mean that the idea of the Experiment has not itself been valid? No. The idea was and is valid. So what went wrong? What went wrong has been previously described.

So what we can do now to close this Summary is to consider one huge correction we can make to begin to correct our course. In the Conclusion we will continue to consider other possibilities.

. . . . .

One of the biggest problems today in the U.S. was again brought to our attention recently in a documentary film called "Food, Inc." I had read about the problem when it began years ago, but this was the first time I had seen a film about it. A quote about the film states: "Food, Inc. lifts the veil on our nation's food industry, exposing how our nation's food supply is now controlled by a handful of Corporations that often put profit above consumer health, the livelihood of the American farmer, the safety of workers and our own environment. Food, Inc. reveals surprising - and often shocking truths - about what we eat, how it is produced and who we have become as a nation."

"Often shocking truths" is an understatement. I could hardly believe the movies of the unhealthful conditions in which the animals we eat are kept in huge "Factory Farms" before being slaughtered, and how their bodies are butchered afterwards.

Just as shocking at the higher level is that "our nation's food supply is now controlled by a handful of Corporations that often put profit above consumer health, the livelihood of the American farmer, the safety of workers and our own environment," and "who we have become as a nation."

As stated in Chapter 9 - The rise of U.S. Corporations, "In defining the term fascism, the American Heritage Illustrated Encyclopedic Dictionary of 1987 describes exactly what has come into being here: *"fascism* - A philosophy or system of government that advocates or exercises a dictatorship of the extreme right, typically through the merging of state and business leadership, together with an ideology of belligerent nationalism." Today we can see that this is exactly what occurred in the nations which started WW II, and that after that terrible war to kill fascism, it has risen in one of the 'victor' nations, the U.S. itself. (Note: That was the last time this definition was included in an American Heritage Dictionary. Now they refer only to Mussolini, Hitler, etc., not to anything which could be identified with the U.S.A.)

Food, Inc. shows how the U.S. Government is working hand in hand with the Corporations to control what crops are grown, by what methods, and in what quantities, for what uses, especially corn, regardless of anything other than profits. Of course, any information about this program is suppressed in the national media, especially about how Monsanto has enslaved the American farmer in several vicious ways, including unwarranted lawsuits against small and medium-sized farmers, and by using the old 'Company Store" technique of forcing them into ruinous debt. The entire "Factory Farm" program is not only anti-American and immoral but anti-human and anti-life.

The reason why I am bringing this up here is that I think we citizens may have to educate ourselves about our invalid system of government and public information, as part of educating ourselves about the larger system which I call The Human Experiment, and that we must begin immediately. Apparently the only peaceful and legal way we can begin is to find competent candidates for Congress who will sign a document pledging themselves, when elected, to... legally and peacefully... *add to our Constitution an amendment which re-states the amendment proposed by Thomas Jefferson and James Madison during the writing of our Constitution.*

As stated, the proposed Amendment would have prohibited "monopolies in commerce," which would have made it illegal for corporations to own other corporations, or to give money to politicians or to otherwise influence elections. Corporations would be chartered by the states for the primary purpose of "serving the public good." They would not possess the legal status of natural persons but of "artificial persons." They would have only those legal attributes which the law saw fit to give them. They could not possess the same bundle of rights which actual flesh and blood persons enjoy. Neither the subsequent 14th Amendment of the US Constitution, nor any provision of that document would protect the artificial entities known as corporations. Although Jefferson and Madison continued to fight hard for the amendment, in the end it was not adopted because a majority of persons in the first Congress believed that already existing state laws governing corporations were adequate for constraining corporate power. What followed shows that they were very wrong.

The moment to correct that error... legally and peacefully... has come, and in fact is long overdue. Please do not imagine or say that we can not do this. We can do any legal and peaceful thing we need to in order to save ourselves, especially our children, and the youth who will be the ones to carry out this vital mission.

In Chapter 3 I asked a question. Do some of our ideas run us? Yes, one especially, which is our wonderful, essential idea that we *need to continually create appropriate ideas.* The essence of the Human Experiment is that we can be better off by creating ideas to guide us, rather than depending on instinct. Yes, we can create them, but they will be successful only if we use Nature as our guide. Our mistake has been to try to have it both ways, i.e. to transcend instinct and *not* create the necessary ideas to replace it. Whenever we discount a natural law that was serving a necessary purpose, we need to replace it by an appropriate human law, and that is what we have *not* done.

Another vital point is that to be able to trust Nature as our guide, we must be sure that its workings are not being invaded in ways which would affect its ability to be our valid guide. Unfortunately, today these working are being invaded by Corporations which are doing "Genetic Engineering," GE. Whether or not this could disqualify Nature as our trusted guide is unknown to me at this time, but the possibility is one more reason for us to regain control of Corporations.

. . . . .

Thus we humans unknowingly disabled our evolved, mental, personal computers by suppressing the new ideas we needed in order to heal our corrupted third-brain Culture, in order for us to create the ideas which would welcome the development, integration, and guidance of the fourth brain. We desperately need this because its "window of awareness" shows that *the only way one can have what one needs and desires is to cooperate with each other person on our beautiful planet Earth.*

We can call this "enlightened *self*-interest," and we have all the information and equipment to respond to it and make our planet into a human paradise for each person living on it.

Unfortunately, too many persons in power today are continuing to fight change and have doubled and tripled the use of their money-power to suppress new, rational ideas, and to spread false, destructive ones, by paying millions of dollars to greedy, professional political liars, and buying and running the media.

Fortunately, education about our actual human situation is being spread around the world in various ways, and hopefully more and more persons will recognize the truth and will stand together against ignorance and tyranny in time to save our species, and our place in our Universe, and our place on our beautiful planet Earth.

Now, on to the Conclusion!

Chapter 16
Conclusion

Today people all over Earth are asking themselves and each other, "Is this the end of our human species, or a second beginning? Have we made ourselves the irrecoverable victims of our own short-sightedness and consequent folly? Has our destruction of our life-sustaining natural environment and of our Human Experiment gone past their points of recovery, or can we use our wonderful brain systems to understand why we are on a suicidal course, and create new ways to save ourselves?"

The conclusion of this book is that our Human Experiment is failing because our ideas stopped evolving. Consequently our third brain Culture became stuck, and subject to being controlled by power-seeking persons.

A purpose of this book is to help provide the information we need in order to create the cooperative ideas which will enable us to begin evolving again, which will cause our Human Experiment to again be successful. This will enable us to recover from our suicidal course and put ourselves on a new cooperative and enjoyable one toward entering the Fourth Human Paradise.

It is now clear that we have enough information to succeed, if we are to have enough time. My concern about having enough time is that climate change (aka global warming) may too soon kill us all, and kill all the other animals and the plants too. However, we now have the information we require to stop global warming, and if we all begin to apply it immediately we can stop it in time to prevent chaos.

I think that our new awareness of the existence and importance of our fourth brain, and of our having stopped its development, is the key to understanding and overcoming our problem.

The reason why is that this halting of its development shows why we humans have been trapped in a non-evolving third-brain Culture for thousands of years, during which time its window of awareness showed us a continuously degenerating picture of our human world, and consequently of the increasingly degenerative ways in which one has had to reason (think) and act in order to survive. That window developed because during those thousands of years of not evolving the third brain and its Culture became more and more corrupted by humans.

An opposite fact of which we must become aware is that during this time many persons actually did develop their fourth brains, and many of them made wonderful contributions, large or small, to our Human Experiment.

However, even though personal contributions are the vital base of the Culture, what we live according to is the *great group of ideas*, the great mass of them, which constitute a prevailing, total Human Culture. Hopefully it is a successful one because it is democratic and just... what we have called a "bright" Culture, in contrast to a "dark" one.

People tell me that of late their conversations always go into the dangerous situations in the entire world now, and that when someone asks what we can do about it the reply is always, "Nothing. We are helpless to have our governments make the necessary changes," and the standard reasons why are given. Well, for the following reasons, we are not helpless!

Sometimes we feel that we are because so many changes have occurred, so quickly, all over Earth, that we humans have not been able to realize that we are living in an entirely new world situation. For example: For the first time, our species has covered our planet and is over-consuming its life-sustaining natural resources faster than they are being replenished.

What is vital for us to recognize is that our deadly situation applies to *everyone*: each person, each family, each tribe, each nation, is faced with our self-destructive global situation.

Even though many persons may feel that our situation is hopeless, and that we are helpless to correct it, the truth is that our situation is *not* hopeless, and we are *not* helpless to correct it, unless we *think* we are helpless. Instead of thinking that, what we can and must *do* is obvious. We must ORGANIZE! Because our problem is global, we must organize globally, and today the good news is that we *can!* That is because for the first time in our Human Story we can see that we can have a....

... CONSCIOUS SPECIES IDENTITY !

What in the world is THAT? The answer is: Prior to becoming human we were *like* the other higher mammals in that we could all form ideas in our brain/mind, but could not communicate them to each other to act on them, because we did not have sufficiently advanced language ability. We were *different* from the other higher mammals in that we had the potential to develop speech. Then we developed it, and rose *above* the other higher mammals because we could use speech to *converse* with each other, and make and carry out complex cooperative plans for group actions.

Because of all this (and because of the biological mutations involved) we can say that we became a new *species,* which we call "human," or "Homo sapiens," (homo = a species of bipedal primates + sapiens = wise).

As wise humans we studied the workings of our Natural environment to discover cause and effect of events, and we began to carry out our Human Experiment. It was *successful* and we had children, and our group grew, and we had to keep dividing it, but all of our children learned to talk to each other, and to create and share cooperative ideas, and to act on them, and these ideas became the human Culture. We passed it on to each new generation who up-dated it to keep up with the changing and evolving survival requirements of the natural environment, and this cultural process continued successfully for a long time.

Thus we were becoming increasingly *different* from all other species of life, and as humans we were creating an *identity* distinct from them, a *species* identity, but were not able to be consciously aware of this. We took it for granted that we were a kind of being better off than all other kinds of beings in that we were the only ones who had speech, which gave us a better group way to survive and to enjoy life. This included (although we could not be consciously aware of it) being able to guide our own personal and group futures through plan-making. We continued to organize ourselves as human groups, and began to spread out over the planet. We could go wherever we liked, because we were superior in cooperative group strength and in weapons.

Then came a basic change in us. While being distanced from each other *physically*, our groups had distanced themselves from each other *culturally*, i.e. had developed ideas and "sub" Cultures different from each others' (such as different clothing, or words, or dialects, or tools, or weapons, etc.) which caused the different groups' members to think and act differently from each other. Consequently, whatever human species identity (or bond) had existed, ceased to exist, and was replaced by feelings of suspicion, fear, dislike, and animosity, perhaps over a natural food territory. That change was accentuated as our groups grew in size and we became tribes, and developed the strong tribal identities which continue to exist today, even within nations. That is why we must ORGANIZE! Because our problem is global, we must organize globally, and now we can. That is because for the first time in our Human Story we can see that we can have a CONSCIOUS SPECIES IDENTITY! To see why we can, we can quote from Chapter 10, titled "Community."

"Regarding the *group,* the design of the new community must recognize that the group includes each person on planet Earth. Very fortunately we have acquired scientific evidence proving that we really are all one group, one species, one ' family.' Comparative studies of blood and of genes in persons all over Earth show that we all have the same ancestry, and that the variation among individuals is so much greater than the differences among groups that the concept of 'race' has become meaningless. There is no scientific basis for saying that any one population is genetically superior or inferior to another. The lack of this knowledge was a main cause of the fall of the first human paradise, and partially a cause of the fall of the second and third ones, and, unless the knowledge is made global, this lack may prevent us from building the fourth one; however, spreading our knowledge that we actually are one family can help us all to work together to create and maintain the fourth paradise by creating appropriate community."

This could be the place in this Conclusion to note that we should perhaps be questioning the success and validity of the type of demarcations we call "nations." To introduce this idea we can recall that after World War One there was created an international body called "The League of *Nations*." The governments of many nations participated in creating and joining it, and several of its divisions, especially The World Health Organization, survived and did much to improve world health. However, as a means of preventing war the League of "Nations" got nowhere. This scenario was repeated after World War Two by The United "Nations" Organization (UN). It seems that the power groups in nations do not desire to give up their sovereignty, and of course the new *inter* national corporations have almost succeeded in taking over the governments of all nations.

On the other hand, it is very interesting to our Story that, in spite of extreme difficulties, 28 nations of Europe (as of 7-1-13) have created a special grouping called the "European Union," have created their own currency (the Euro), and are now creating their own language (based on the two predominant languages, English and German), and have named it Euro English. The plan includes making improvements periodically in English language spelling.

A surprising thing is that organizing globally may be the easiest, quickest, and best way to begin to organize locally. That is because peoples might feel less threatened and even more secure and even excited about joining with the others around the world who have been standing up for freedom and democracy! Almost everyone knows that it is only through real democracy and full global and local cooperation that we can save ourselves today. So to survive what we can and must do now is form ourselves into small, dedicated groups all over Earth whose participants will meet together to write, or to record vocally, descriptions of the actual facts of our *human* situation, and of what we can do by working together. We must spread this information in as many ways as is possible, e.g. by word of mouth (including cell phones), by local newspapers, telephone, radio, TV, the new hand-held electronic communication devices, and whatever. Also we must see that all this is now possible because at long last we can now have what we need to go global: A CONSCIOUS SPECIES IDENTITY!

My idea is that, having reached the higher mammalian goal which had been inspiring and guiding us, we now need another goal to inspire and guide us, and that this goal is... the one we had *originally*.

To see this original goal we need to ask and answer a question: "What does the individual human desire?" My answer is: "Immediately after being born, to become successfully in control of their own life." To a newborn baby that means by crying and having its need for food met immediately by being offered its mother's breast and sucking milk.

As the baby becomes a child, its human desire to become successfully in control of its own life will be met (hopefully, as it was in the human beginning) by being brought up in a democratic Human Community where, during its stages of development, it will learn how to become successfully in control of its own life *in human society*. An old African saying is: "It takes a village to raise a child."

Prior to beginning this Conclusion, I was thinking about using it to attempt to create a Plan by which we humans could save ourselves, and suddenly I have realized that we already have such a Plan!

It is here in plain view to be seen. It is no one person's plan, and at the same time it is everyone's Plan, because it is an evolved one, a resultant one, a derived one, made by all of us. We began it on the east African plain a million years ago. We knew instinctively and consciously that we each needed each other desperately in order to survive, so our Plan had to include each person in our group, and had to be desirable to each one of us, and therefore that it had to be created by each person working together with the others. So we created such a Plan, and used it to reach our goal of inventing The Human Experiment and putting it into practice successfully.

Now we have come full circle. We are again in the situation we were in when we lived in east Africa. We are surrounded by danger, this time in the form of anti-human ideas which we must overcome. However, now we know consciously that in order to survive, our Plan (i.e. our human government... our Culture...) must again include each person in our group, and must be desirable to each one of us, and therefore must be created by each group member working together with the others.

Something *new* is that we are now aware that we must build our Plan of human government *inside* the Natural Plan of Government, which obviously our first ancestors had to do because they could not have done otherwise. A crucial reason for letting Nature be our guide is that everyone can *trust* it, precisely because it is *not* manmade. (In fact, Nature is our human government, and always has been, and today we are being forced to recognize this and to again follow it as our guide.)

Also of vital importance, today we know that our "group" is composed of each person on our planet Earth, because it has been established as a scientific fact through global blood comparisons and gene comparisons, and brain size, and ability, etc.

Therefore we can see *consciously* that we *have* the Species Identity we need today on which to re-establish our original Human Goal, and our original Human Plan and Human Experiment to attain it, and can organize ourselves globally to save ourselves. We desperately need all these in order to see each other as *friends* all over our planet Earth, in order to create a Global Community through which to make and carry out cooperative group plans of action to protect ourselves from the hard time which almost certainly will come before we can recover from our past (and present) mistakes. We can begin now to prepare for whatever will come, and we can see that our basic identity is as humans, and that we must plan to see that each person will have food and our other necessities so that we can all find ways to live out our lives during the hard time, in peace and at least relative happiness.

If we all use the many tools that we have inherited and created we can not only survive, but develop and integrate our *four* brains and build and live in the Fourth Human Paradise, because we are the only species which can control its own destiny, and we know that our fourth brain, thanks to its *wisdom*, will show us two things: not only that the only way for us to survive and enjoy life as persons *is to cooperate with each other person on our planet,* but *will us how to achieve that,* because it is the sapient (wise) part of Homo sapiens.

So now our present generation is facing the ultimate test of the ability of each and all of us as members of our Human Species: Either we will carry out the Human Experiment and Plan, or we will completely stop evolving, and suffer increasingly as persons on our way to extinction, and let evolution select a more worthy candidate to inherit the wondrous paradise on Earth that could have been ours.

Every person I have met who experienced the WW II London Blitz said that, in spite of the hard part, it was *the best time of their lives* because of the way everyone came together and cooperated.

Friday nights at 8:30 there is a program on PBS in Medford, Oregon called "Immense Possibilities" which is getting better every week. The host, Jeff Golden, will tackle anything, and has people of all ages from everywhere come on in person or by television. It is only a half hour show, but during it they cover an amazing amount of people-projects which are helping to solve our problems, including involving our kids... and in each case building trust and cooperation are the basis of success.

Let's find out what we are really made of. With all of our billions of brains working, and creating and exchanging ideas all over our planet, who knows what Immense Possibilities we might come up with, especially now that we can each be in immediate personal communication with each other electronically!

Think of the many fascinating new friends we can make! Let's see if We the People can overcome our problems by joining together in a new global movement to spread the facts, especially because of our growing awareness of the danger to all of us being caused by our previously blind destruction of our life-sustaining Natural Environment. As the host of Immense Possibilities says at the end of the program, "Please do what you can do."

I will, and I believe that you will too!

Closing Note: Writing this book has helped me greatly in overcoming the effects of PTSD, and I hope it can help others too.

I thank all of the wonderful persons who have helped me during my lifetime. I regret that we all continue to be subject to the miserably corrupted Third Brain Culture and I hope that this book can help us to correct it, and to create the Fourth Human Paradise.

Best wishes, Jim

PART III
Breakthrough

Knowing Our Place in the Universe

Chapter 17
Breakthrough

The reason for adding Part III - Breakthrough, and this final chapter with the same title, is that we humans have at long last created the ideas which enable us to break through the barriers that have kept us from being able to make our Human Experiment again successful.

Arranged in the order of most overall importance to us, a list of these barriers would have to begin with those which prevented us from knowing about our Universe.

1. Thus, *the first essential idea* we all need to know about today is the *Nature of our Universe,* because everything has resulted from it. Very fortunately it has been made easy for us humans living today to have the background information necessary to understanding this idea basically, thanks to the popular work of the late Julian Huxley. He described our Universe as being a single Process of Change, that we call "evolution," which is occurring in three main phases. In this way he connected Lyell's basic ideas about the *non-living phase* of the evolution of our Universe, to Darwin's basic ideas about the *living phase* of the evolution of our Universe, and then connected both of these to his own basic ideas which recognize a *human phase* of the evolution of our Universe, and that its method of change is through the human creation of ideas and their being passed on to each new generation in the form of a transmissible Culture. That gave us the complete basic background of the Universal Process of Change that we call "Evolution," and showed us our human place in it, and how we participate in it.

This is vital for us to know, because we must participate in this Process of Change in order to make our Experiment successful; otherwise, we will not evolve, and will continue on our self-destructive course.

2.   *The second essential idea* is that being shown our *place* in the evolution of our Universe enables us to know when our Human Story began, and to follow it from then into the present time and see what happened along the way. Gaining this information has been vital because it shows us our successes and mistakes, and how to correct the latter.

3.   *The third essential idea* is that in our human beginning the evolution of our ideas occurred *naturally* in our brain\mind, because we based them on the workings of our surrounding, evolving, natural environment. This successful situation continued for a long time, but then we began to form ideas *not* based on our surrounding, evolving, natural environment, and consequently they, and the (third-brain) Culture they formed, could *not* evolve. That took us off of our successful course and put us on the self-destructive course we have been on ever since.

4.   *The fourth essential idea* came from the late neuro-scientist Dr. Paul Maclean, former chief of the Division of Brain Evolution and Behavior at the U.S. National Institutes of Health (NIH). He recognized that the three brains in our head correspond to the evolved brains in the heads of the three main stages of animal evolution: reptilian, old mammalian, and new mammalian, and he described them. He recognized and described also a *fourth* evolved brain in our head (behind our frontal brow), which did not begin to develop until some 40 thousand years ago and has not yet completed its development because of humans suppressing the necessary new ideas. We desperately need its development to be completed now, because it will be the smartest brain and can guide all four brains in the ways essential to us. Most importantly, it can show us that the only way one can have what one desires and needs is to cooperate with every other person on our planet.

5.   *The fifth essential idea* relates to our need to recognize the two-part desire that begins when we are born and guides us throughout our lifetime. One part of that desire is to eat, in order to survive, and the other part is to successfully gain control of one's own life, in order to be able to enjoy it. The newborn baby begins to fulfill both parts of this desire by crying until it is offered the mother's breast, grabs it, and begins to suck milk. To continue to fulfill both parts of its desire the baby must be able to grow up in a viable human

community, which must be created and maintained by its parents and other adults cooperating.

6. *The sixth essential idea* is that the first human government was democratic, because it is the Natural form of human government, and the only form that can be successful for us. Today that means *Constitutional* Democracy, and where possible *Direct* Democracy, i.e. with each person of age participating personally.

7. *The seventh essential idea* is that the initial and basic mistake made by the first humans (but which they could not help making) was to begin to create an "artificial" human government of ideas, before being able to recognize that a "real" Natural Government to which they were subject already existed. For their ideas of human government to work, they had to be created and applied *inside* the Natural Government, and in support of it. Not knowing this, they built their human government *on top of* the Natural Government in order to control it, and, in many ways they and their descendants began to destroy it.

   (It is interesting to note that in one way they began properly, which was to study the workings of their surrounding natural environment in order to discover the causes and effects of events, so in this way they were studying the Natural Government. However, they were not yet sufficiently evolved to see that the workings of their natural environment *were* their natural government. We, their modern descendants, are only now making the connection, and are suffering greatly because it has taken us so long to do so! I am of course referring to our human destruction of the vital elements of our life-sustaining natural environment, when instead we should have been supporting them; the result is that today we are suffering the terrifying effects, the most recent being the onset of climate change, i.e. killing ourselves by polluting the planet's atmosphere.)

8. *The eighth essential idea* is that, because we could not recognize that we were subject to a Natural Government, we could not recognize that whenever we cancelled a necessary Natural Law, we needed to replace it by creating a human law.

For instance, before we humans emerged on planet Earth, Nature had been keeping a balance between the number of living things on our planet, and the amount of food necessary to support them, (partly) by having animals killing and eating each other so there was no over-population. However, after humans emerged and developed mentally it seemed to them that Nature's way of achieving this balance was too savage to apply to them, so they invented ways to keep from being killed. This would have been a logical move if they had known that to keep what had been the natural balance they would have to invent an artificial way of keeping it. Finally, safe and easy ways to prevent pregnancy have been invented, but it took so long that human population kept growing and growing until now there are far too many of us.

World population in:
   1804 was 1 billion;
   1927- 2 billion;
   1960- 3 billion;
   1974- 4 billion;
   1987- 5 billion;
   1999- 6 billion;
   2011- 7 billion.

Projected for 2030- 8 billion; for 2050- 9 billion, and pregnancy control has still not yet been adequately applied.

Actually, the first humans sometimes had to abandon infants and old persons because they could not be carried. Later, groups such as herders which had to keep moving, did learn from experience that a mother could keep nursing to avoid pregnancy. Other ways involving hunter\ gatherer groups have always been abstinence and infanticide. However, sedentary agricultural groups thought a mother could have as many children as she could feed.

9. *The ninth essential idea* is that the main reason why we have not applied our vital ideas is that the knowledge of them has not been presented, or not presented properly, to most humans, and in many cases has been consciously and purposely kept from them.

Because of a lack of the necessary public education, most persons on Earth have not even been told our actual Human Story, so we have unknowingly interfered with the development and integration of our children's' brains. The result is the dysfunctional human world of today, because our brains form different, incomplete, inaccurate pictures of our actual human situation, and can not form a picture showing that we can all survive and enjoy life by cooperating. This problem can be resolved now, because we have the means to give all information to everyone everywhere. A system will have to be invented to present the information so that it can be understood quickly by each person, perhaps by categorizing it.

10. *The tenth essential idea* is that we Americans need to continue publicizing a vital truth about our U.S. government and our economic and financial systems. In Chapter 9 we began to state this vital truth by noting that during the writing of the U.S. Constitution Thomas Jefferson and James Madison, two of the new nation's greatest statesmen, were well aware of the danger of powerful corporations. They knew that the American Revolution was in substantial degree a revolt against the tyrannical domination of colonial economic and political life by the greatest multinational corporation of its age: the British East India Company. Therefore Jefferson and Madison worked diligently to have an 11th Amendment included in the original Constitution to join the other ten amendments which together are known as the Bill of Rights.

The proposed Amendment would have prohibited "monopolies in commerce," which would have made it illegal for corporations to own other corporations, or to give money to politicians or to otherwise influence elections. Corporations would be chartered by the states for the primary purpose of "serving the public good." They would not possess the legal status of natural persons but of "artificial persons." They would have only those legal attributes which the law saw fit to give them. They could not possess the same bundle of rights which actual flesh and blood persons enjoy. Neither the subsequent 14th Amendment of the US Constitution, nor any provision of that document would protect the artificial entities known as corporations. Although Jefferson and Madison continued to fight hard for the amendment, in the end it was not adopted because a majority of persons in the first Congress believed that already existing state laws governing corporations were adequate for constraining corporate power. What followed shows that they were very wrong.

To repeat part of the description given in Chapter 9:

After the ratification of the Constitution by the States, some persons thought our country needed heavy industry in order to make its place in the modern world. Large amounts of funding were needed and to raise them the federal government and the states' governments issued charters for private persons to form corporations which would be considered artificial persons, with the understanding that they would be monitored closely and prevented from doing anything not serving the public good. This surveillance was necessary because in a capitalist system a corporation, having no brain, mind, or conscience, is a robot (computer) programed to make as much money as possible in the shortest time for its officers and investors, regardless of the effect on anyone else.

For 100 years after the U.S. Constitution was ratified, state and federal officials watched the activities of corporations closely and revoked their charters immediately if they went against the public good in any way. However, during that time railroads were continuously expanded, in the east and westward, and the railroad corporations became increasingly rich and powerful. Consequently their attorneys kept bringing cases into courts to get them to say that corporations were real persons and entitled to those rights. President Abraham Lincoln recognized what the corporate attorneys were seeking and consequently he wrote: "I see in the near future a crisis approaching that unnerves me and causes me to tremble for the safety of my country.... Corporations have been enthroned and an era of corruption in high places will follow, and the money power of the country will endeavor to prolong its reign by working upon the prejudices of people until all wealth is aggregated in a few hands and the Republic is destroyed."

Unfortunately his dire prediction has almost come true, beginning with a criminal act by an attorney, formerly a railroad corporation's president, who took the matter into his own hands. Acting as a court reporter, in 1886 he wrote a summary of a court's action (called a "headnote") involving Santa Clara County and the Southern Pacific Railroad Corporation in which he said the court had given the corporation the Constitutional rights of a real person. The court's official record shows that this was a *false* statement, but using this criminal loophole corporations quickly began to do things very much against the public good.

The results for us Americans are that several of our corporations, along with those of other nations, have become global, have grown to enormous size, and being robots with no brain, mind, conscience, or morality, are being used by their officers to become the modern day agents of the Dark Culture, over-consuming or destroying our life-sustaining natural resources, and systematically destroying our Constitution and our democratic way of life as fast as they can in order to increase their corporative powers and profits.

It comes close to committing "the perfect crime:" the corporative structure is a robot programmed to follow the rules of the accepted capitalistic system, so the CEO's rationalize that they are innocent of any wrong-doing, and so do the stockholders. Members of Congress do nothing to stop this crime, because they receive large amounts of corporative money to use for their reelection, and eventually for them to become lobbyists for the corporations (called "the revolving door").

Some examples of corporative crimes, among many others, are that they have used the huge corporative fortunes to: take over and genetically alter the world's food supply; drive small and medium sized farms out of business; buy and corrupt our national media; rig our elective process; hire thousands of corporate representatives called "lobbyists" to influence our Congress to write legislation favorable to Corporations, including those which profit from wars; and, assisted by their servants, those radio and television commentators and newspaper writers who twist information and promote fear and hatred, have created an atmosphere which, under the guise of fighting "terrorism," has resulted in a step by step process of taking away the rights guaranteed to us by our Constitution. Hence the almost incomprehensibly, terrible fact is that our government, and consequently our personal lives, are being run by the agents of a *robot.* By telling gross lies these agents have made it into a horrible, murdering monster, using its power and money to cause the waging of oil-and-empire-seeking wars which have killed many thousands of innocent civilians and several thousands of our American soldiers, and wounded or maimed many more thousands of civilians and soldiers, all completely unnecessarily.

This insanity began during the presidency of George H. W. Bush. (Continued in Chapter 9.)

This tragic account of a corrupted USA could go on and on (and does so in Chapter 9), but the purpose of its being repeated here is to allow me to say that we should do now what Jefferson and Madison knew we should have done over 200 years ago, which would have prevented all of the horror which followed the refusal by the first Congress to add their amendment to our original Constitution. But better late than never, so I am asking the American people to demand that our supposedly democratic Congress ADD THE PROPOSED AMENDMENT NOW!! Before it does become too late!

The End... And the New Beginning

Partial List of References

The Declaration of Independence of the Thirteen American Colonies, 1776

The United States Constitution

Food, Inc. - A Robert Kenner Film, 2008 Magnolia
Pictures Unequal Protection

The Rise of Corporate Dominance & The Theft of Human rights; Thom Hartman; Rodale 2002

Big History: From the Big Bang to the Present, Cynthia Stokes Brown, The New Press, 2007

When Corporations Rule the World, David C. Korten, Kumarian Press & Berrett-Koehler Pubs. 2001

NOW with Bill Moyers - PBS TV 1\03 Guest "Chuck" Spinney, formerly with Pentagon.

Evolution in Action; Julian Huxley; Harper & Brothers 1953

Knowledge, Morality, and Destiny; Julian Huxley; Harper & Brothers,.1957

The Biology of Transcendence; Joseph Chilton Pearce; Park St. Press, 2002

Consilience; Edward O. Wilson; Alfred A. Knopf 1998

The Moral Animal; Robert Wright; Vintage Books, Random House 1994

Bertrand Russell's Best; edited by Robert E. Egner; George Allen & Unwin Ltd., 1958

The Origins of Virtue; Matt Ridley; Viking 1997

This Is Biology; Ernst Mayr; Belknap/Harvard 1997

Cosmos; Carl Sagan; Random House 1980

This Changing Earth; Samuel W. Matthews; National Geographic 1/73

Atlas of World History; Rand McNally; 1983.

A Brief History of Science; Consultant Editor John Gribbin; Barnes & Noble Books 1998

The Elegant Universe; Brian Greene; W. W. Norton & Co., Inc. 1999

Life On Earth; David Attenborough; Little Brown 1979

Biological Science; William T. Keeton; W.W. Norton, 2nd Ed. 1972

The Selfish Gene; Richard Dawkins; Oxford University Press 1989

Origins Reconsidered; Richard Leakey & Roger Lewin; Doubleday 1992

The Survival of the Species; Richard Leakey; PBS TV 12/83

Becoming Human; Ian Tattersall; Harcourt Brace 1998

The Baby Book; Sears & Sears; Little Brown & Co. 1993

The Demon-Haunted World; Carl Sagan; Ballantine Books 1996

The Dragons of Eden; Carl Sagan; Random House 1977

The Procession of Life; Alfred S. Romer; World Publishing 1968

The Human Revolution; Ashley Montagu; Bantam Books 1967

The Immense Journey; Lauren Eiseley; Random House 1957

The Population Bomb; Paul Ehrlich; Ballantine Books, NY 1978

The Population Explosion; P.& A. Ehrlich; Amicus Journal Wntr/90

Man's Presumptuous Brain; A.T.W. Simeons, MD; E.P. Dutton 1962
The Meaning of Anxiety; Rollo May; W.W. Norton, Rev. Ed. 1977
The Oil Depletion Protocol; Richard Heinberg
Background for Man; Dolhinow & Sarich; Little Brown 1971
The Emergence of Man (Series) Time-Life Books:
   The Missing Link; Maitland A. Edey; 1972
   The First Men; Edmund Whits & Dale M. Brown; 1973
   The Neanderthals; George Constable; 1973
   Cro-Magnon Man; Tom Prideaux; 1973
   The First Americans; Robert Claiborne; 1973
   The First Farmers; Jonathan Norton Leonard; 1973
   The First Cities; Dora Jane Hamblin; 1973
Man: an Autobiography; George R. Stewart; Random House 1946
Man Makes Himself; V. Gordon Childe; Mentor Books 1951
The City in History; Lewis Mumford; Harcourt, Brace & World 1961
World's End Series; Upton Sinclair; 11 vol, Viking etc. 1940-1953
A History of Europe from the Reformation to the Present Day; Ferdinand Schevill; Harcourt, Brace 1946
Small Is Beautiful; E.F. Schumacher; Harper & Row 1973
The Turning Point; Fritjof Capra; Bantam Books 1981
Guns, Germs, and Steel; Jared Diamond; W.W. Norton & Co. 1999
Corporate Culture, Paul Cienfuegos, Sentient Times April, 1999
Speech on history of corporations given by Richard Grossman, 1997
The Greening of America; Charles A. Reich; Random House 1970
The Making of a Counter Culture; Theodore Roszak; Doubleday 1969
The Decisive Decade; Don Hinrichsen; The Amicus Journal Wntr/90
Media Virus!; Douglas Rushkoff; Ballantine Books 1994
It Takes A Village; Hillary Rodham Clinton; Simon & Schuster 1996
The Evolution of Cooperation; Robert Axelrod; Basic Books 1984
The Family, Prison of Love; Phillippe Aries; Psychology Today 8/75
From Mondragon to America; Greg MacLeod; U Cape Breton Press 1997
Basic Formula to Create Community Supported Agriculture; R. Van En, CSA Indian Line Farm, Great Barrington, Mass. 1988
The Integral Urban House; Farallones Inst; Sierra Club Bks. 1979
Secrets of the Soil; P. Tompkins & C. Bird; Harper & Row 1989
We Own It: Starting and Managing Cooperatives and Employee Owned Ventures; Honigsberg, Kamoroff, & Beatty: Bell Springs Pub 1991
Communities Directory - A Guide to Cooperative Living; Fellowship for Intentional Community, Langley WA 1995, etc.
Communities - A Quarterly Journal of Cooperative Living; various; Fellowship for Int. Com., Route 1, Box 155, Rutledge, MO.
In Context - A Quarterly Of Humane Sustainable Culture various; Context Institute, Bainbridge Island, WA.
The Holy Bible; Thomas Nelson & Sons 1929
The World In Literature; Vol. One: Backgrounds of the Modern World; Warnock & Anderson; Scott, Foresman & Co. 1950

A History of Philosophy; B. A. G. Fuller; Henry Holt & Co. 1946
The dictionary of Philosophy: Dagobert D, Runes; Philosoph. Library, NY 1942
The Lord of the Rings; J. R. R. Tolkien; Houghton Mifflin 1965
Harry Potter Series; J.K. Rowling; Scholastic Inc. 1998
The Power of Myth; Joseph Campbell & Bill Moyers; Doubleday 1988
United Nations Publications
World Book Encyclopedia
Encyclopaedia Britannica
Encyclopedia Americana
Webster's College Dictionary; Random House; 1997
The American Heritage Illustrated Encyclopedic Dictionary, Houghton Miflin 1987,
Webster's College Dictionary, Random House, NY 1997
Webster's New World Dictionary; The World Publishing Co. 1962
Webster's New Collegiate Dictionary; G. & C. Merriam Co. 1949
Newspapers, news magazines, TV programs, lectures, etc.
Bill Moyers' Journal, and David Broncaccio's "NOW" - PBS TV
Charlie Rose, PBS TV

USAGE NOTE: I think this note is important to writers and readers. I have encountered two related problems continually and found them to be a hindrance. The first problem is in needing to refer to both sexes. The second problem has to do with the uses of singulars and plurals.

Recently I found the solution to both problems In Webster's Dictionary in connection with the word "they." It stated the following. "*Usage:* Long before the use of generic HE was condemned as sexist, the pronouns they, their and them were used in educated speech and in all but the most formal writing to refer to indefinite pronouns and to singular nouns of general personal reference, probably because such nouns are probably often not felt to be exclusively singular: *If anyone calls, tell them I'll be back at six. Everyone began looking for their books at once.* Shakespeare, Swift, Shelley, Scott, and Dickens, as well as many other English and American writers have used they and its forms to refer to singular antecedents. Although rejected as ungrammatical by some usage critics, this use of their, they, and them is increasing in all bu the most conservatively edited American English."

Under the word their, Webster's states: "2. Used after an indefinite singular antecedent in place of the definite form *his* or *hers. Someone left their book on the table.*"

www.ingramcontent.com/pod-product-compliance
Lightning Source LLC
Chambersburg PA
CBHW070803280326
41934CB00012B/3036